Books should be returned on or before the
last date stamped below.

A Desert Rat in Holburn Street

Autobiography of Duncan McGregor
Illustrations by Rhoda Howie

All Good Wishes
Duncan McGregor
30/3/94

ARDO PUBLISHING COMPANY

I am grateful to the Tank Museum of the Royal Armoured Corps Centre, Bovington Camp, Wareham, Dorset for their kind permission to reproduce the photographs of tanks. I am also grateful to Aberdeen Journals for their kind permission to reproduce the photographs on pages 109, 135

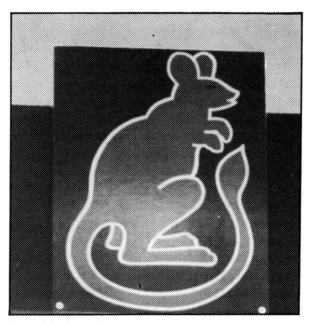

Logo of the Desert Rats

Badge of the First Royal Tank Regiment

Contents

Duncan McGregor

Preface

I SUPPOSE the reason why I wrote this book is one of the oldest in the world - I was asked to do it. I love talking to people, and it served me well throughout my life, and was always appreciated.

In the course of many conversations, I spoke about the War, and about building the peace, and what small parts I had played in both. Many folk suggested that I should think about putting it all down on paper - a kind of history of war and peace by an ordinary North-East 'loon'. With their encouragement, therefore, I have chronicled the events of what, for me, have been exciting and rewarding years.

Lest any should think that there was any suggestion of boasting on my part, let me assure the reader that I look back only with gratitude and humility. I was never a boastful person, and I owe a debt to comrades, colleagues and friends, which these pages can never begin to adequately express.

I have written from memory alone, and the events I record are perhaps only a small part of the host of experiences, joyful and sad, I have been spared to share. The war years have to be from memory alone, since we were forbidden to write diaries, or have a camera. Not that I would need such things, for the places and faces are forever etched in my mind, in a way that time itself could never erase.

I am not a writer of books, and former 'writing' was limited to ledgers and records of business, rather than to any kind of personal reflection. I owe a special thankyou to a very good friend for his help and encouragement.

I thank God who has spared me to enjoy so many happy and busy years, especially when I look back to times when it was natural to believe that days were numbered and life could be tragically cut short.

I humbly dedicate this book to family, friends, customers and colleagues - to my dear comrades of those dark days, and to the memory of those who were not spared to share the peace.

Duncan McGregor
Aberdeen, 1993.

CHAPTER ONE

My Early Years

MARKET HILL, a small community in Glass and some seven miles from Huntly, is remembered with great affection by all who look back to the old days. With its grocer's shop, shoemaker and joiner, it will always have a place in my heart as the village of my birth. I was the youngest of three children, with an older sister and brother, and we were a close and happy family with a loving mother at its heart. When I was four, we moved to the grocer's shop and post office in Kinmuck near Inverurie. This was another hamlet like my birthplace, but with the exciting addition of a blacksmith's shop.

    One of the unique features of Kinmuck was a Quaker meeting hall and burial ground. Every year a large gathering occurred when the Quakers spent much of Saturday in the hundred year old hall. In the graveyard, all the stones were identical save one, and although this did not please them, it seems that this was a matter over which they had no control. The burial ground could always be recognised for the mounds of earth all about since it was the practice not to remove earth from the graves.

    It was easy to while away the hours out of school either with Peter Anderson at Sunnyside farm, or John Spark at Wardhead farm. The joiner, blacksmith and shoemaker all had shops within a hundred yards of our house so I was used to popping in for a chat, or to watch them at work. I never needed Lego toys since I got all the off-cuts from the joiner, and it was great to watch the smith fashioning the horseshoes, all the while avoiding the sparks from the anvil as he shaped the iron into shoes. I can still smell the hoof as the iron shoe was pressed against it, and I can almost see still, the shoemaker shaping the edge of the sole with a small piece of hot iron on a wooden handle. He would then use some black substance which made the sole lovely and shiny. The feeding and milking at the farms was always a fascinating adventure, and I never remember getting the feeling that I was in the way or being a nuisance.

I told of the annual Quaker meeting at the hall, and I recall what a fine group of people they were. While their

The blacksmith at work

meetings were private, I don't remember them having a pastor, and they kept themselves very much to themselves.

Winters were awful hard, and the road from the shop to the school was often blocked with drifts up to 12 foot high. There were no snowploughs in those days, and the neighbours would eventually group together and shovel their way through -

a hard job since the snow had to be thrown some distance clear. For us children, of course, the snow made a welcome visitor, with snowball fights, sledging and sliding. We could skate along the tracks made by the cars, and the blacksmith would always give us a piece of iron to fit on our sledges. Sadly, these days have passed, and I cannot recall in recent memory snowfalls quite so severe.

As the years passed, we got a football pitch at Fawells, although the goalposts were not of Hampden Park standard, since Keithhall didn't provide trees of that calibre. Still, we didn't mind, and football gave us fun and exercise, and we held dances in the village hall to raise funds for our team called Keithhall Blue Bell Athletic. There was never any nastiness, but I found it difficult to keep up my interest and pleasure in the team when I went to Inverurie Academy. When I left the academy and moved to Bainshole, that was the end of my football experience.

The Keithhall Games were always a highlight, with all the sideshows such as Aunt Sally with the clay pipe in her mouth, the sandbags we had to hit through a hole in a piece of wood, the shooting and the races, plus jumping and pillow-fights on the horse. All the local lads took part, and there were events for the ladies to show their skills as well. Afterwards, a big dancing board was laid down, and the jigging went on into the wee sma' hours. For all the fun, I took special joy in the spoon race and the three-legged events, all of which enriched the fun.

I began my schooling at Keithhall Public School, some one and a quarter miles distant, where around seventy pupils were taught by Miss Thomson, Miss Laing and Mr Taylor. Outwith school hours we had our own household duties to perform, as well as chores in the grocer's shop. Father went out in his van to serve the good folk of the district around with groceries and other general goods, collecting eggs from the farmers to sell in Aberdeen. These were responsibilities which demanded hard work, and very long hours. What homework we got took very little of our time, and it was amazing how we always managed to find lots of things to do to amuse ourselves with our pals. Looking back to those days, it seems as if scant attention was paid to education, and I often recount how I was never lower than fourth in my class - a class of four.

As I passed into Mr Taylor's room, the head teacher advised my parents to send me to Inverurie Academy for my last three years of schooling. Since the academy was 4 miles from Kinmuck, I became the proud possessor of a bicycle, which I lovingly cleaned and oiled every weekend. I soon discovered that Inverurie Academy was a world away from Keithhall in terms of school-work, with many more subjects and far higher standards of expectation than those to which I had been happily accustomed. The pressure was terrific, in terms of school and homework, but over those three years I managed, with sweat and toil, to arrive in the top seven in classes of thirty five. The grand result of these efforts was the Day-School Certificate, and I cycled home from the academy on my last day with my wheels scarcely seeming to touch the ground.

I find that life, as one passes through it, is filled with horizons, so that when one is reached, another is just coming into view. For me, this newest horizon meant finding a job, which could be difficult in this rural community since I had no experience of farmwork. The school had been notified of a vacancy for a junior clerk with Kellas, the solicitor, and both myself and my pal, Norman Fraser, were put forward. I was unsuccessful.

My uncle, John Simpson, came to the rescue. He had a licensed grocer shop in the Glens of Foudland, and it was a blessing that, when he learned that I had left school and was looking for work, he invited me to work for him. Having little choice, I was glad to accept the offer and came to Bainshole. Since it was about twenty miles from Kinmuck, I would only be able to go home for a weekend every three weeks or so.

CHAPTER TWO

The Working Loon

ATTACHED TO the shop was a croft which was cultivated, so
I worked on the land on my half-days. It possessed a horse, a
cow and three young cattle, so my day began at 6.30 in the
morning, helping with the animals before breakfast. I was in
the shop at 8.30 am, preparing goods pre-packed for the delivery van, all of which was a fairly hefty start to each day. I
worked in the shop until 9.00 pm every day except Wednesday,
and it wasn't long before I was relieving my uncle of all shop
duties, much to his delight.

    The Glens of Foudland was a wild place, and it was said
that in the winter time, if there was a snowstorm, you just had
to sneeze to block the roads. During these rough winters, my
uncle and I would go round the houses in the Glens with a
horse and sledge. When the snow was level with the tops of the
fences and dykes dividing the fields, we would take the sledge
over the top of them. With straw in one box to collect the eggs,
and the other boxes filled with the necessities such as salt,
bread, flour, sugar, and cereals for making soup, it was some
journey. Talk about being frozen?

    However, the winters passed and the summer days
arrived again. Dances were held in the Glens of Foudland
school, and we did the catering for them, which meant my
being in the shop at 10 o'clock at night, even after a 5.30 am

rise. Being licensed, of course, the farm lads aye needed some 'oiling' before the dance, and their custom was regular and brisk.

It was not always a pleasure, although my uncle was as good a soul as you could find, quite unlike my aunt. For instance, we were up at 5.30 am one Friday morning, loading the van with eggs for sale in Aberdeen. After we cared for the animals and had breakfast I would be in the shop at 7.30. My aunt had washed part of the floor while I was getting things ready to load the van again when it came back from Aberdeen. As I stepped over her hands, she roared "You wee devil, you step over my hands once more, and I'll slap you round the face with this floor cloth."

What a lovely start to the day, and there was no reply for it seemed that no matter what I did for the good of the business, I never got any appreciation from my aunt. I did the buying for the shop, and I remember an invoice which arrived one dinner time from Hutcheon of Turriff. We bought almost all our heavy goods from them, such as a ton of cattle and hen food, and half a ton of sugar, all of which they delivered without charge. I can remember my aunt looking at this particular invoice and saying "It's well seen the person who ordered all that doesn't have to pay for it."

My uncle John tried to help me out by saying that if we didn't buy the goods we couldn't sell them and make any money, but this underlying current of ill-will from my aunt always made me feel uneasy. Another nastiness concerned the van man, Hector, who had been at Bainshole for a few years, and reckoned he would step into the business. I suppose he saw me as opposition, being related to the owner. We both slept in a bothy room adjoining the house. Being a restless sleeper, my legs would wander over to Hector's side of the bed, and many a time I was awakened by his kicking me. We never held any conversation, although I carried all the goods out to the van for him to load. If my mother had known this it would have angered her, so I suffered in silence.

The shop was the social centre of the Glens, and it was good of an evening to hear the local lads relating the tales of the Glens. In those days, a farmer was considered prosperous if he bought a bicycle, and some even had cars, although these were usually old bangers. At 9.00 pm, when I made moves to close up, they would all suddenly remember what they had come for, such as maize or cake for the cattle. There was no point in getting het up about this, for it was all in the day's work, so it was a case of then counting the cash and getting to bed.

We were to have a new bothy built, and my uncle bought

Duncan outside the Bainshole shop

an old railway carriage for Hector and me to sleep in. We spent a whole winter in this lodging. Bainshole was low-lying, and a burn flowed past us. The frost in winter was intense, and before we went into the carriage at night, I took a stone with me so that I could prise my boots from the floor in the morning. Still, we survived, and before you wonder if there was no room in the house, there were six rooms, but Aunt Mary wouldn't be bothered with us being in the house causing her extra work. Most of the Glens folks knew what she was like, but I had a job, and the princely sum of £2 every three weeks. Although I had my board, Mary was never a great spender, and two pounds of beef lasted four of us from Saturday to Tuesday, with stovies on a Wednesday. It didn't do us any harm, though, and we had the occasional treat of a half-pound of liver.

The farmers of the Glens were a fine lot, with one or two real worthies, like Johnnie Hay whom I shall never forget. When the amber liquid was flowing freely, he would perhaps have a wee drop too much. We would all tease him about how he would catch it when he got home. "Naw, naw" he would reply, "I'll be alright. I'll jist wait until she's speechless." I'll always remember the expression on his face and the ever-present tin of snuff, pinches of which were apt to match the number of drinks he had. Still, it was all in good part.

Another job I had on the croft was to deal with the growing menace of moles, and I appointed myself molecatcher. Although I had no experience, I found it quite easy to set the traps, and I was given an allowance for every mole I caught, though I forget now what the reward was.

Although my aunt was nasty, I still took in the coal for her, and saw to the feeding of her hens, plus any other jobs she requested. I'll never forget her final farewell to me on the morning I left to start the egg business. I was cleaning my shoes, and getting ready for Cameron the carrier's lorry to take me to Inverurie. She came in from the byre, and addressed these well-chosen words to me: "I don't know what you think you're doing. There hasn't been a McGregor successful yet, and I don't think you'll be any different." There was no reply to that, and I still don't understand what makes people so nasty. I had never spoken back to my aunt, and had tried to do everything to help the place and the business. I don't know what satisfaction it gave her, but I must admit that whenever we had a poor day selling the eggs, her words came back to me. You know it's easy to say that we should simply forget things like that, but words can never be taken back, no more than can an unkind act. At least I know her prophecy didn't come true, for I have no idea which McGregors were unsuccessful, and I know of none who ever paid less than twenty shillings in the pound.

The days and years passed, and I can't say I ever felt sad or lonely. There was always someone calling in for a dram, and I got to know all the folk for miles around, which was just as well seeing I was never out of the shop except for my week-ends home.

CHAPTER THREE

A Man of Business

I HAVE mentioned my egg business, and it came about this way. It was during one of my few weekend trips to the family when I heard that young Smith, the Kintore grocer's son, was selling eggs in Glasgow and doing very well. My brother, who had been serving his time in a garage in Inverurie, had fallen from his cycle on a slippery road. He unfortunately fell into the path of a steam wagon, and badly damaged a leg and arm which forced him to quit his apprenticeship. After six months in Aberdeen Royal Infirmary, and with only partial use of arm and leg, I wondered if we might both try our hand selling eggs in the south.

Since father was able to collect eggs from the neighbouring farms, we had a ready supply. With the seeds of hope planted in my brother's heart, we advertised in the *Glasgow Herald* and the *Falkirk Herald* for a store to accommodate a van and fifty egg boxes. We had no replies from Glasgow, but offers came from the Falkirk district, and we decided to take a store in Larbert. Fortunately, one of our neighbours had an aunt in Stenhousemuir who took boarders, and Mrs Esplin was delighted to have us.

Now we had our store and our digs, so we proceeded to purchase a serviceable van at Cheyne's in Great Western Road in Aberdeen, for £65. Now came the hard part. I had to tell my uncle what I intended to do. With a lump in my throat, I broke the news to him one day when we were alone in the Bainshole shop. As I told him that George and I intended to go south, to rekindle my brother's interest in life, he was speechless. The tears running down his face almost melted my resolve, but I felt that this was in my brother's best interests and that we had to do it. We had the van painted white, with

"ABERDEENSHIRE EGGS"

written boldly on the sides. Though my pennies were few in number by this time, I spent £4 to insert an advertisement in the *Falkirk Herald*:

"Look out for the white van with the fresh Aberdeenshire eggs! Guaranteed graded and tested"

The egg van

What good that did us is hard to tell, but at least it was good for our morale. Three weeks from the time we had first spoken about the idea, we were on the road with twelve 30-dozen boxes of eggs which cost £2 per box. Imagine that, 'one-and-fourpence' per dozen. Still, we managed to pay £24 for our stock and set off from Kinmuck for the unknown, myself a lad of 19 and my brother 25. Never having been south of Stonehaven, the journey broke new ground and we arrived in

Larbert in the early afternoon. We inspected our store, then found our lodgings where we settled in during the rest of the day.

Bright and early on Tuesday morning we set off, with me at the wheel and our hearts in our mouths. Where on earth did we start? We decided to begin with those houses on the edge of the town of Larbert, and I shall never forget my very first call at the lodge which was fifty yards from Larbert Cross. Armed with my basket of eggs, that was my big moment. You can imagine how I felt when the man of the house, listening to my pitch, replied "Och, laddie, I keep hens."

Later I knocked at a door in Larbert and the lady opened her upstairs window. When I had introduced myself and said "Would you like to buy some fine fresh Aberdeenshire eggs?" came the reply "What do you think you're doing down here taking away folks' livelihood? We've plenty of eggs here." I didn't have a reply ready. Luckily it wasn't the end of the world, and we proceeded to canvass both sides of the street.

There were other hazards; some of the cottages had an enclosed back door and many of them had a notice on the gate 'No Canvassers, No Hawkers, No Tramps, No Bills'. I didn't know which category applied to me but I never dared to force an entry. At some time, when I might have seen the occupier at a baker's van I did take the opportunity to tell her about my nice fresh eggs from Aberdeen, but I cannot recall any success. Another nasty notice on some of the gates was 'Beware of the Dog'. Would I or wouldn't I? Had we persevered and been bitten, they wouldn't have taken any responsibility. One day I was walking towards the back door of a council house when a Shetland collie came at me and almost tore my shoe off. It was such a bad tear that I couldn't keep my shoe on when I walked. I didn't think I needed this sort of problem when business was none too plentiful.

Sometimes what started off as a disaster had a pleasant ending. I knocked at one lady's door and before I said more than a few words, she gave the door such a bang it just about cut my face off. I can't really tell how it happened but within a few weeks this same lady came to the van and asked if we would call. She bought three dozen eggs every week and that was a big order for an ordinary household. And we were quite certain that no other egg seller would ever get her order, for if she applied the same treatment I received to others, there was little hope of anyone going to her door again.

Embarassing moments came sometimes when we were knocking on all the doors. I would knock and while I was waiting for the lady to come to the door another seller would stop his car or van at the gate, take out a basket and come and join me on the doorstep. This was obviously his customer and all I could hope for was a big hole to open up and consume me. Eventually we knocked on every door in Larbert, Stenhousemuir, Carron, Plean, Bainsford, Grahamston, Falkirk, Camelon, Denny and Dunipace, Grangemouth and Polmont. It was hard work, but it was amazing just how quickly our contacts grew into customers. We were so glad when we met folk with Aberdeen connections, and these were almost always winners for our wee business.

When we had set up our business in these areas, we turned our attention to Kings Park in Glasgow. On our first day, having worked from 10 am until 4 o'clock in the afternoon, we had sold exactly £1 nine shillings worth of eggs. By the time we had really developed this outlet, we were making a profit of between £5 and £6 per day. All this at a time when the workers in the foundries and works were earning about £3 in a week.

Our business was building steadily, and the white van we started off with had served its purpose so we invested in another. We went to Lanark to see a Bedford van which belonged to a butcher. He was giving up business so we got a good deal and it served as long as the egg business was viable. Every four weeks or so we made a point of sharing the weekend with the folks back home. One such visit occurred during the weekend of 3rd September, 1939......

CHAPTER FOUR

A Call to Arms

IN COMMON with all who heard it then, I shall never forget Chamberlain's broadcast telling us that we were at war with Germany. For some moments there was silence, as the terrible news filtered into our hearts and minds. We could only wonder what the implications would be for us as a family. There was a general feeling of patriotism, but I couldn't help wondering in a very personal way what would be my lot.

I volunteered for the Royal Armoured Corps, which had been my father's unit in the First World War, and which he had survived. I was not called immediately, though, and I had to bide my time anxiously. My brother was, of course, unfit for active service, but he anguished for me and the rest of Aberdeenshire's young folk. At length my orders came, to report to R.A.C. Menin Lines at Catterick Camp on 1st August, 1940, and I left my brother to carry on the egg business on his own.

Believe it or not, I had no idea what R.A.C. stood for, and there was no-one who seemed able to enlighten me, so it was to be a journey of discovery in every sense. I remember only too well the day of my departure, and it was a heart-heavy one. My dear mother, who had always seen to our spiritual upbringing and needs, now reminded me of the words of the Saviour she had served so well - *Be not afraid, for I am with you always, even to the end of the world.*

The words certainly seemed appropriate, for as I made my way to Aberdeen station, I felt that the end of the world, as we had known and loved it, might very well be nigh. My drooping spirits were lifted a little when the train came into Stonehaven and I was joined by Jock Craib, the grocer's son from Rickerton. It transpired that we were both headed for the same place, and more Scots lads joined us along the way before we arrived at Brandon station.

When we eventually found Menin Lines, we realised what R.A.C. meant as we saw the huge metal monsters with their gun barrels sticking out. I remember that shiver which ran up and down my spine, almost as a premonition of terrible things to come. Anyone foolish enough to harbour notions about being non-combatant was quickly disabused as we looked in awe at these fearsome weapons of war. However, one has to accept one's lot, and there was a war to be won.

By the end of the day, the seventy or so Scots chaps had been divided into two squads, those with surname initials A-L in the one, and M-Z in the other. We were soon issued with uniform and equipment, and the last signs of freedom were gone, creating a sense of gloom all around. Jock and I were in different squads but our introduction to drill was the same as the army did its best to change us from raw civilians to toughened fighting men.

If this was hard, the injections were worse, and the side-effects quite startling. The physical training was strenuous to put it mildly, and the drill intensive, but we were gradually transformed into a bunch of extremely fit soldiers, with new skills in first aid and map reading. After these three weeks of torture, attention turned to driving lorries with a view to the army's determining who would be drivers and gunners, and who would train as radio operators.

Eventually sixteen of us were chosen as drivers, and after a short course on gunnery and radio operations, we were trained in mechanics. After two weeks of intense training, there was a change of plans. Eight of us were sent home on embarkation leave. On our return we were issued with tropical kit, and it didn't take an Einstein to guess what area of God's good earth we were to explore. By December we were on the move to Liverpool quay where Brittania was berthed. I spent the waiting time wondering how on earth I could avoid going abroad, especially by sea. However, it was up the gangplank that New Year's day, 1941, and that was that. Did I hear someone say "Happy New Year"? We sailed on 3rd January away north-west round the coast of Ireland - a convoy of eight great liners with a naval escort.

For the first few days, I passed the time in my bunk, since this seemed a sensible alternative to being terribly seasick every time I tried to get up. Most of us were the same but it soon passed, to be replaced by the most dreadful boredom. Apart from boat drills there was little else to do, so we spent most of the waking hours playing cards and secretly wondering what awaited us when we reached our destination. As we made our way down the west coast of Africa, the weather became much warmer. But our joy at this was short-lived when our ship developed engine trouble and the convoy left us. What a chance for some marauding submarine to pick off an easy target, and there were some anxious hours until we got under way again.

It was a great moment when we docked at Durban, and the four afternoons of shore leave were spent with delightful folk and good food. It seemed no time before we set sail again, heading for Port Said and the desert. All we seemed able to see as we disembarked was an endless horizon of sand, much of which was transferred to us by the churning of the transport vehicles which picked us up. At length we arrived at a tented camp and were immediately divided into four groups. When I found myself in a different group from my pals, I did a quick swap, and only later discovered that I had changed from H.Q. to 'A' squadron. The awful significance of my mistake will be revealed later.

Meantime, we were allocated to tents, and issued with

three blankets, mess tin, knife, fork and spoon. We learned quickly how best to use the blankets to afford the best comfort on cold, hard sand. We discovered that the unit we had reinforced was the 1st Royal Tank Regiment which had just returned from the highly successful Wavel push. Although the Italian tanks had been knocked out, three squadrons of the regiment remained at Tobruk surrounded by German divisions.

Besides the discomfort of the sand, the heat was oppressive and the flies legion, but we simply had to learn to put up with it as best we could. In due course the Matilda infantry tanks arrived, each weighing fifty tons and powered by two 8-cylinder diesel engines, and bearing 2-pounder guns. Equipped with machine guns firing 1200 rounds per minute, the armour plating was three to four inches thick. We were four to a crew, being tank commander, driver, gunner and radio operator. Conditions inside were very cramped and it was no place to be if you suffered from claustrophobia. The driver had his own perch but the other three had to do as best they could in the restricted space.

In addition to crew, room had to be made for sixty to seventy 2-pounder rounds of ammunition plus twenty-six boxes of ammunition for the machine-gun, with each box containing belts of 250 rounds. We had to wear headsets at all times since the noise made normal voice contact impossible. The tank commander and radio operator were obliged to remain on air for orders, although the commander could switch to internal communications as required. The driver and gunner were on an internal communication link at all times.

It wasn't long before tank crews were detailed, and when I was posted as gunner, I approached the sergeant-major saying that a mistake had been made as I was a driver. Sergeant Major Alexander replied "You'll get a course." This wasn't worth thinking about in the middle of the desert and I didn't take the matter any further, just in case my motive was misunderstood. Though I didn't fancy this assignment one little bit, I reckoned someone had to do it, so why not me? The driver was Jock

Cameron from Glasgow while the radio job went to Trooper Warburton, and all three of us worked hard on our tank. I even learned to strip and clean the guns - with more than a little help from my friends.

I had never fired a gun during the brief gunner's course at Catterick, as only those already selected as gunners were given firing practice. I was not at all happy about this omission as I would dearly have preferred a lot of instruction on handling and firing before going into action. I had to take a crash course on traversing the gun, lining up and firing on targets, and use of the handle which operated the powered turret to turn left or right. The trigger was incorporated in the traverse handle, along with safety catches for the two guns. It would not be easy to get every action co-ordinated but gunners were expected to be able to fire on the move - rather difficult if the tank was moving across uneven ground. Our only vision was through a telescopic sight which had range markings and cross wires for aiming.

The driver and operator had vision through a visor measuring about 4 inches by 2 inches when the tank was closed down. When it was too dangerous to poke his head out at the top of the vehicle, the tank commander had visors in the top of the copola. I knew I had little chance of practice while the tank was stationary in base, but I was pretty sure there would be plenty of opportunity when the time came for us to move to the front. That time came all too soon.

CHAPTER FIVE

The Short Route to Hell

AT THE beginning of May 1941 we were on the move. All our excess clothing such as shorts, shirts, underwear and socks were packed separately. This was fine but the packages were kept on a lorry which was never less than twenty to thirty miles from the front. Aboard the tank we had our three blankets, mess gear and one change of underwear - plus a revolver.

We moved our tanks to the train-flats which were no more than reinforced boards and yet were able to bear the load of 50-ton tanks. One minor detail perhaps, is that those flats had to bear us as well, since we ate and slept on them along with our tanks. During this move I was afflicted by sandfly fever and couldn't eat anything during the four or five days journey to Mersa Matru. There was no doctor available and any attempt to report sick might have been badly misunderstood. Upon arrival we parked in a circle and the advance party provided a meal for us of bully stew, some sliced peaches and carnation milk. It was the first nourishment I had seen in six days but all I could attempt was the peaches and milk - which I off-loaded the next day, totally undigested.

The next shock came when we were sent out in our vehicles, as I thought, to get some gunnery practice at imaginary targets. We were issued with lorry sides to camouflage the tanks, and since these sides were fixed to the guns, that put paid to any kind of practice. We travelled at 5 miles per hour for several days, stopping only occasionally for a brew-up. Before we left, we put together to buy £60 of food - tinned fruit, sugar, milk, tea and tinned meat (not corned beef). Although we didn't make much use of these stores - since we hoped to get something a little more tasty when we had the chance - the £15 I paid put me in debt since my pay was a mere ten shillings per week.

One morning, around daybreak, shells started to land all around us and the lorry sides were taken off. Things were pretty tense as the shells continued to drop but it would have been out of place for our turret gun to be turning. Some of our other squadrons went into action that day and got a pretty hot reception. Our task was to provide cover protection for the infantry and to hold Fort Cupuso. Zero hour for us came at 4.30 in the afternoon and as we were on the startline a Royal Artillery officer came into our tank. His job was to direct shelling at the enemy wherever they were, and he checked with Radio-Operator Trooper Warburton that the set was transmitting. This was essential so that he could relay orders to his artillery gunners. For some unknown reason the set would not transmit although Warburton tried frantically for some time with no response whatsoever.

The officer couldn't wait, and jumped off our tank to cross to another some 40 yards away. He hadn't even reached it before our radio started transmitting. The commander from the other tank crossed over to us and we were on the move. What a feeling of apprehension, stark fear and yet anticipation. I can remember it vividly even today. As we trundled forward I suddenly thought of the folks at home getting the tea ready. Thank God they didn't know what was happening here on the other side of the world. With eyes anxiously flicking from side to side, we reached the Fort which turned out to be just rubble with no action and no enemy in sight. We moved on and suddenly, about a hundred yards away, hundreds of German infantry, complete with backpacks, rose and ran as fast as they could. The commander gave the orders "Gunner action. German infantry - 80 yards - FIRE!"

The gun was blazing fire at 1200 rounds per minute, as I traversed it from side to side, guided more by the tracer bullets than the ranger. All at once our tank shook as a shell crashed into it, but we moved on and the Germans rose and ran again. Now tanks appeared and I took the same fire orders from the commander firing shell after shell. The tank commander shouted "You've hit it! Hit it again!"

I tried to oblige and the infantry continued to retreat before us. We were hit again and again by anti-tank shells - crunch after crunch shaking the tank, and we couldn't understand what was happening. A dispatch rider came across our path, and the fire orders barked out "Dispatch rider - passing our front at 100 yards - FIRE!"

The Matilda infantry tank

I just kept firing across his route until he ran into the bullets. Everything was happening. We were firing machine-gun bullets almost continually between shelling tanks and armoured cars. The heat in the tank was 120 degrees and the telescope was dripping with condensation as the sweat poured from my chin. The smoke from my guns filled the tank but we were so close to the enemy that we had to close down and were in effect in a sealed box.

A shell hit us. It passed the driver and smashed the batteries so it was a blessing that the engines were diesel. We moved this way and that as we continued to be hit with anti-tank shells. One shell actually came through the body of the tank at my feet, and we began to wonder how on earth we could survive this onslaught. Then another shell hit the gun cradle and took a chunk out of it. All at once the gun cradle on my shoulder took a jolt and faced into the ground.

As an attacking force we were finished but we still had to stay and take what was coming. Now I could hardly believe what I was seeing, as a solid line of German tanks counter-attacked. We tried to turn around but it was a slow business and we weren't even sure where the shells had hit us. Our tank came to a halt as it became apparent that our engines had been hit - thirteen times in fact - causing them to seize up.

We had to bail out. As we hit the ground machine-gun bullets whizzed all around us. We ran for our lives and it was fortunate for us that the light was beginning to fade. As we ran towards our rear position, a tank approached and the driver told us he was looking for a crew - commander, gunner and radio operator. We clambered aboard and were met by an unbeliev-able sight. A shell had drilled through the 3 inch turret killing the rest of the crew and flesh and blood spattered the inside of the tank. The smell of death was strong - the blood and charred flesh - and our commander decided we could not possibly engage the enemy in these conditions.

We moved back until we came to one of our own replen-ishing lorries where I spent a very uncomfortable night being nipped by the stack of petrol cans it carried. By the next day, however, we were out of the frontal area and only then heard that the tank which had gone into action with the artillery officer, had been hit with the loss of all crew. What a thought - that if our radio had worked in the first place, it might well have been us.

Indeed, there was a lot of hard thinking by now. Thousands of miles from home, there seemed to be very little future for us except more of the same hazard and heartbreak, with the inevitable finale. Recalling this first brush with the real horror of war made me tremble for no words could ever describe the shock and terror we experienced. How could mankind resort to such depths of behaviour? I had no doubt that I had been the cause of suffering and death to many infantry lads that day. Even if they were German - and enemies - they were mothers' sons like us. Even as I had fired, I had no thought of killing but rather obeying orders in the midst of war. The reality, with all its terrible and tragic meanings, preyed heavily on my mind.

It was strange but living in the desert didn't bother us so much any more, and even the flies and heat had lost their first impact on us. Best of all was the fact that we were to enjoy a short but welcome taste of civilisation before we returned to this inferno again.

CHAPTER SIX

Living Dangerously

WE WERE soon on our way back to civilisation and barrack
duty at Alexandria. We were to spend some two months here
before returning to the desert and the next call to arms. In that
two month period we were allowed four days leave for which
we had to go to the barracks in Cairo. It was always a source of
irritation to us that we were required to pay our own train fare
from Alexandria to Cairo. It had been some two years since I
had enjoyed any leave and to have to pay for it seemed a bit
harsh to say the least, especially since the service folk at home
had leave every few months, with travel paid. Still, it was good
to be free for a while, and my first night on a real bed made me
feel I was floating on air.

When this tour ended, things were to be very different.
We were to be taken to Tobruk by sea to join up with the
members of the original battalion. All our possessions had to
be stowed in one pack - clothes, blankets, the lot - making us
feel like donkeys, although they might have coped better. Our
boots had to be packed as well since the order was to wear
gymshoes for the voyage. We boarded H.M.S. Kingston, a
destroyer, in Alexandria harbour. The lads on board were doing
a regular run to Tobruk and told us that with a "bit of luck"
we'd be in Tobruk by midnight. We sailed about 8.00 in the
morning, a few destroyers and an escort of 2 ack-ack ships.

Most of our voyage took us along enemy coastline so that we were almost constantly under observation. Attack from the air was almost continuous, and as we stood scattered around the decks we saw first the yellow ensign and then the red, signalling imminent danger and action stations. I was standing below what was called 'Chicago pianos' - a nest of twelve guns firing simultaneously with the resulting deafening noise. The ships were doing a zig-zag pattern at about 28 knots causing the waves to reach what seemed no more than a foot from the decks.

We escaped being hit but Tobruk harbour was under attack as we approached, which seemed to be a nightly occurence. We negotiated the wrecks in the harbour and tied up, giving us the blessing of getting onto terra firma at last. With packs on backs we marched for several hours with only a very few breaks. It was a real effort to get the packs off and then throw them on again, and the body heat was evident from the bar of chocolate in my shirt pocket which quickly became no more than a brown stain. There was always a shortage of food in Tobruk, since the NAAFI supply ship only came about once a month, and when ships were sunk it was odds on the NAAFI ship was one of them. Even when it did get through, my allocation was likely to be no more than a bar of chocolate and a tube of toothpaste.

Our destination where we joined the rest of the lads was a big empty patch in the desert near a landing-strip, with the tanks dug in around it, and our boys well entrenched in underground bunkers. We had repeated drops of leaflets telling us we were about to be attacked by land, sea and air and advising us to give up. A few days after the drop, three huge troop-carrying planes descended toward us from a height of five hundred feet. One of them almost had its wheels on the ground when the ack-ack guns opened up. It hurriedly took off again followed by the other two. They all got away.

We lived with sandstorms and flies. Our food was scarce but our army biscuits were augmented by small amounts of bread from a bakery in Tobruk. It looked like raisin bread, except that the raisins were weevils. Still I never saw any bread thrown away as we made do with anything and everything. Smokers were issued with 50 Victory-Vs per week and I gave mine to Jock Nicol from Cumnock though I could have sold them for £5. Evenings were spent in my dugout, and fruit cakes I had from home were shared one slice each night - something we looked forward to.

It seemed obvious to us that we had to free Tobruk, and we agreed that if anything happened to one of us, the other would write to the family. When the push came, Jock's tank commander was Bob McGregor from Elgin, a great chap with

Last war tanks at Tobruk

so much knowledge and wisdom. Their tank was only one and a half inch armour-plated with a 2-pound gun and machine-gun. Mine had half to three-quarter inch plating with a .3 and

.5 Vicker machine-gun. In terms of weight my tank was 15 tons while Jock's was 35 tons. These were last war tanks and it was such a waste of good lads - especially our 1st Battalion Royal Tank Regiment men - although *we* didn't matter so much.

When the attack began we were all involved, with the heavier tanks doing the stickier business while the light tanks were protecting the flanks. There were thousands of mines laid in and around Tobruk. Some were charted while others had been laid by the infantry mostly for their own protection. Since the light tanks had only half inch plating on the floors, a mine strike with the left track would lose the bottom of the tank, the battery and the driver's leg or legs. In that event death would occur within four to five days since the blood, affected by poor nourishment, couldn't enable the body to fight germs.

I was on guard duty one morning when there were bursts of machine-gun fire. I woke the lads and three tanks were sent out to investigate. Half an hour later they were back, but another Jock from Glasgow had lost his left leg. He was brave and cheerful but his fate was sealed. Then came news that my pal Jock Nicol had been killed by a shell through the front of his tank. My heart broke, and I found it impossible to believe I could ever escape this carnage. I pulled myself together, for duty had to be done and it wasn't ours to reason why. There had been a heroic act by Bob McGregor, Jock's tank commander, who had carried six wounded tank crew to a running tank even though he was ready to collapse. Some remarked to Lieutenant Blaistow that Bob deserved a Victoria Cross for this, but so many brave acts like this were too easily ignored as if it was only what was expected of us.

It was later in 1942 when Gus Holiman took over as our squadron commander that he learned of Bob's bravery and Bob was awarded the military medal for his courage.

Our troop of three small tanks was sent out to locate the enemy rather than use the infantry. We completed our mission without any sightings but rather stupidly stopped within 10 yards of each other. I discovered two broken track-pins, which could so easily happen. They were repairable, and I was working away when a chap from another tank sauntered across and said casually "Would you look at those planes..."

I well remember saying something to the effect "Never mind the planes. Let's get on with the war effort." when seven German stukas broke formation and zeroed in on us. I jumped into the driver's seat and had just closed one flap when I was showered with sand and stones from the first bombs. The scream of the stukas was just hellish and all we could do was huddle in our tanks, fingers crossed, as we were rocked by one explosion after another. We didn't see how we could survive this as they attacked us four times. It was almost unbearable with the noise of the bombs and the scream of the planes.

I'm quite sure the pilots must have reported three enemy tanks destroyed, such was the chaos all around. Three of the lads caught outside the tanks had been wounded, and there was a crater just three feet from us in which we could have buried our wee tank. We couldn't bring ourselves to move until we had brewed a cup of tea, and from the biscuit tin behind the driver's seat I extracted the last of the fruit cake which poor Jock and I hadn't finished. It tasted like the food of the gods.

We returned to join our squadron, and the next afternoon as we sat watching the Germans, I was told to take the tank back and check it thoroughly as I was to take an R.A. observer officer out next day. I did a complete check of tracks, oil, water and battery before the officer arrived at 4.00 am next morning complete with his blankets. When we were loaded I tried to start the engine - no start. I tried to get a tow from another troop tank but first my tow-rope and then his broke. We finally had to get a tow-rope from yet another tank and this time we were successful. The officer couldn't wait and went to find another tank as we resumed our usual duties. Next day the news came that the officer and the tank crew which had been substituted had all been killed. Once more I realised that had it not been for two broken tow-ropes it would have been us. First the radio at Fort Cupuso and now the tow-rope, so would it be third time lucky or unlucky?

The battle continued for days until the force coming west from Egypt took the pressure off us. As I had promised him I would, I sought and received permission to write to Jock Nicol's wife and give her the sad news. It was the first notification she had, and whether it was more acceptable than the official letter from the War Office I did not know. The shock was devastating no matter how the news was delivered. I had promised to visit her, but it was five to six years after the tragedy that I made my way to Old Cumnock.

Many thoughts passed through my mind during the journey, and I paused outside the village to think how I might best approach the visit. It wasn't finding words which worried me so much as what effect my presence would have on her. Had she re-married and if so would her new husband be there? What would they think about my belated visit and would they realise that it was the result of a solemn promise made? I wondered about trying first to find her mother or even Jock's mother. Yet again my visit might be opening the wounds again at a time when perhaps they were coming to terms with their loss. For better or worse I did not go ahead with my promise, although someday I may make tentative enquiries about my pal's family. I shall just have to be guided by my own conscience if and when that time comes.

Our tanks were no match for the German Mark IV's with their 75 mm guns and thick armour. By the time we returned to the delta and Cairo area, Christmas had come and gone without our noticing it. It was said that it took nine men at the back to support one man at the Front, but I often wonder why I had to always be the *one* instead of one of the nine. When we did return to Cairo we were loaded on trucks and taken some 15 miles from the city. With one tap supplying the squadron with shaving and washing water, there was little of comfort without even a canteen to make ourselves a cup of tea.

We got out of camp two afternoons a week but walking about five miles before hitch-hiking was not much fun. Since our unit couldn't supply transport, we relied on other units for a lift, but we still enjoyed those breaks. It was so good to have a change of food and showers, which we often enjoyed three times in one afternoon because of the heat.

Light tanks of the 1st Royal Tank Regiment

CHAPTER SEVEN

No Time for Practice

WE WERE supplied with tanks again which we parked beside our tented area. We were termed the 'Light Squadron' and we had as reconnaissance tanks the American Honeys, weighing 25 tons with a 7-cylinder radial engine and armed with a .37 machine-gun. We were three Scots and an Englishman in our crew, and our instructions were - "Here are your tanks - get on with it."

We got the theory of the engines, which didn't require much maintenance, being air-cooled and thus eliminating a lot of possible troubles. A trial exercise was set up for the end of May, to give us a chance of working together and getting used to the tank's performance. Wednesday 27th May, 1941 was my birthday and happened to be a day we were allowed out of camp. That afternoon I think everyone was out apart from those on duty. The usual procedure of getting away from camp and back again applied, and most of us got back after midnight. Under the present conditions, however, that didn't present a problem. We had hardly got under the covers when George McKeown, much the worse for drink, came round the tents banging a petrol can with a stick shouting "Wake up! Wake up! There's a flap on. Get your kit together."

Soon the orderly-sergeant followed with the official orders which told us to have our kit packed and outside the

tents as soon as possible. We had to draw our emergency
rations, machine-gun ammunition and stretcher as soon as
possible. The light of day found us armed with 30 belts of 250
machine-gun rounds to fill and boy were our fingers sore. By
afternoon we pulled out of our area to put our tanks on the
train-flats, and once again we were on our way to the barren
wastes, reaching the rail head within a few days. After unload-
ing we travelled a further few miles before parking in the usual
formation - H.Q. tanks in the centre with the other twelve tanks
forming a circle around them.

Before long a tank commanders' meeting was called at
the squadron commander's tank. Our commander had left us
and his replacement was a Regular tank officer, Captain Thom.
When he came back from the meeting he suggested a cup of tea
before explaining to us that we would be in action in half an
hour. We were flabbergasted, and I'll never forget the fear on
the faces of Charlie and John; mine must have been the same.
The last engagement had been our third and we had begun to
realise what it was all about. Enemy columns were advancing
toward us and Captain Thom was in charge of our three-tank
troop. Orders came over the air that our three tanks were to
lead ahead of the other twelve. We engaged, and one of our
tanks was knocked out by anti-tank fire but thankfully the crew
bailed out.

We had survived the first brush, and when we stabilised
and then withdrew from the Front at sundown, the tanks
formed a line of protection for the replenishment vehicles
during the night. The tanks needed to be refuelled and re-
loaded each night, and it was usually about midnight before we
completed our tasks and were issued rations of tea, milk, sugar,
corned beef and army biscuits. We had to be up and ready half
an hour before light at about 4.30, and between midnight and
then had to take our share of guard duty as well. The pressures
were very real, with lack of sleep and then being enclosed in
our tank for about 18 hours a day. This, along with the stress of
attacking and being attacked, all in such high temperatures,

took its toll.

By 4.30 am we had our orders to lead the regiment to contact the enemy. Since the troop commander was in our tank, we were at the front, followed by the other remaining tank of our trio and the twelve tanks of our squadron. We were at least 100 yards ahead of the rest when we contacted the enemy and our squadron formed a line of visual contact with the Germans.

The forenoon passed and it was obvious that Captain Thom was the keen type, anxious to get on with the war. Our tank alone went back to Regimental H.Q. and the use of maps and protractors signalled that something was being planned. Our front line was along the top of a ridge overlooking a four square mile area of level ground. In the distance about two to three miles away was an escarpment of higher ground but still covered with sand. The commander signalled that we were going on alone since it was too dangerous even to take another tank. We crawled slowly along the low ground and came across a Royal Artillery observation officer with his tank.

After an exchange of information, we proceeded towards this higher ground and Captain Thom said "McGregor, do you think you can take us up to the top of this hill?" More with bravado than courage, I replied "Nae bother," and so we proceeded up the track to find ourselves on what looked like the top of a table mountain. Not a soul was in sight, only one of our British tanks which had been knocked out a short time before. Thom and I crawled up to inspect this tank and only then did the captain admit that he hadn't expected to make it up the hill "Mac," he had said, "I expected to get shot up, going up that hill."

We found what little remained of an officer and I suggested that we bury him, but Thom said we should look around a little first. I crawled to the edge of the hill and got the shock of my life. About 150 yards away German infantrymen were sitting by their trenches cleaning their rifles and smoking. Thom wasn't happy with this either and we decided to play it cool and stay in our tank. All at once, however, shells began to crash around us and since no one else was in sight it seemed clear that we were the target. About 40 shells came at us - the term for ten rounds gunfire from four guns. There were a few near misses, so Thom ordered us to remain in the tank hoping the enemy would believe that we had been put out of action.

As the light faded we were still two or three miles from our regiment, and the captain said bluntly "It's up to you, McGregor. You'll have to get us back as fast as you can through enemy lines." It was a rough journey. At twenty miles per hour, I had to spot trenches and weave around them even though poor light prevented any real vision. We got back safely, and I realised that if this was a taste of what was expected of us, it was going to be very dangerous times indeed. After the usual broken sleep it was dawn again, and again came the orders "AZOB TWO! PROTECTION FRONT!" I truly wondered if I would ever have the experience of seeing a tank in front of us.

Observation of the enemy began again, and I knew that this was rather tame for Captain Thom. He ordered us back to H.Q. and we thought "what next?" Back we went again to our line of tanks and our dear captain announced his intentions. "Now McGregor, we're to draw fire from the enemy to locate their gun positions. Drive as fast as you can in their direction." He had worked out positions and we advanced straight at them. At speeds of 20 to 25 miles per hour, we led the way with our second tank 50 yards behind and to our left. When we saw the flashes of enemy guns we had to turn round as fast as we could. The captain gave me general directions and I did some twisting and turning so that a weaving pattern would make a harder target for the enemy. I obviously succeeded in denying their guns a chance to aim properly and we survived. Later in the day, the heavy tanks came into action while the lighter ones kept the flanks protected against enemy action from the rear. We lived another day.

At nights we took what little food we could get or wanted, though a good hot cup of tea would have been far more

welcome. Then we sought a smooth piece of ground to put
down a blanket before finding out where our guard replacements were sleeping. Our day always finished with a prayer of
thanks.

Once again it was back to the front and again our officer
told us to draw the enemy's fire, never being content to just
watch and observe. I was not a brave person by any means, but
Captain Thom possessed such qualities of leadership, that we
trusted him enough to do exactly what he told us, with some
confidence. I was beginning to make a fine art of this twisting
and turning pattern with the tank, while Thom obviously
possessed skills for tanks and desert warfare. After some
sorties had been completed he said "McGregor, I don't know
who taught you to drive a tank, but I've never seen one handled
the way you do it. Mind you, if you knew how many shells just
missed us, you'd get a shock." I took the first part as a compli-
ment, but preferred not to think about the second.

The pattern went on, with us drawing fire at least once a
day. We were almost glad when the heavy tanks went into
battle since it meant we could pause in the midst of our death
missions. We were spending eighteen hours a day in our tank,
only getting out again at nightfall. One day, however, Thom
had another idea and asked me to advance as slowly as possible
so as not to raise dust. The radial engine was not supposed to
be idled, but I had no option. Taking our other tank with us we
moved forward about a mile from our front line and spotted a
line of German tanks so close that I could count 35 of them in
all. We could see the Germans, sitting beside their tanks having
a smoke, but we were as yet undetected. I let Charles our radio
operator have a quick look through the visor, and he almost had
a fit. Thom asked me if I could make a quick dash 100 yards
forward, and I was just suggesting that we were near enough
when I saw the enemy tanks starting up. Thom told me to right-
about as fast as possible, but with all the engine idling I
couldn't get speed from the tank. I simply made as much dust
as possible and somehow we made it again.

Commanding our other tank in the troop was a sergeant who had been a commando. I asked him what he thought of what we were doing and whether it was worse than being in the commandos. "We had a chance at least," he replied, "that bugger will get us all killed." We had been doing a regular pattern of sorties for twelve days now and our reconnaissance activity told us that a full-blown attack was imminent. When we returned to night formation at length, a tank commanders' conference was called.

American Honey tank

CHAPTER EIGHT

The Knightsbridge Affair

THE ATTACK was to be launched next morning at 8.30, and that was the only day we were able to have hot tea and proper food in over two weeks. That is quite true, for if we didn't get an army biscuit inside the tank before leaving in the morning, we got nothing all day. I tried to have a water bottle with me, but it would have been awkward if we had to bail out. How we existed I shall never know.

I folded my blankets into a kind of sleeping-bag and used my boiler-suit on top of my boots as a pillow. We only slept because our bodies screamed out for rest. The morning of the attack we were up at 4.30 and used our petrol fire to make tea while trying to save a little water for our water bottles. Then it was a quick check to make sure all was in order and I made sure the engine governor was off since it restricted us to 1900 revs when we needed 2400 to give more speed for twist and turn. Zero hour arrived and we moved toward the enemy with the words in our ears that if we knocked out 90 German tanks we'd soon be in Tripoli. That was all very well, but the enemy was not going to stand back and allow us such successes easily, so we knew full well that some bloody times lay ahead.

As usual the morning orders came "AZOB2! PROTEC-TION FRONT!" With our tank leading and our second some 50 yards behind, while the remainder of the squadron followed

100 yards behind again, we advanced. I received orders to speed up, go left and advance another 150 yards, when flashes of gunfire appeared about 80 yards ahead of us. I used to say it was like the Blackpool illuminations but this was no pleasure trip.

I knew this was it, and that with all this gunfire, there was no way we could escape. Sure enough, the tank stopped, and I told the commander that we'd been hit. He ordered us to bale out, and we put into operation what all drivers had been practising for such eventuality. Two flaps had to be opened which had been closed down for the attack. I baled out first, followed by the gunner who was at my back, then Charlie Bissel the radio operator. Captain Thom baled out from the top of the turret and we cleared the tank. There was an infantry trench about eight yards away, but I felt that was too near. Our tank, meanwhile, was hit again and was on fire. Our other tank came towards us to make the pick-up but we were under a hail of machine-gun fire and couldn't get off the ground.

Then our other tank was hit too and set on fire. Our original troop of three had been completely wiped out. Our heavy tanks were still about 800 to 1000 yards away, and were already coming under attack by anti-tank fire. The shells which were aimed at them zoomed over us, and it was terrifying just lying there in the open amid this deafening noise of anti-tank and machine-gun fire. As the anti-tank fire abated, there was a splash of machine-gun fire right in the middle of us, like a boiling pot and within inches of each man. John and Charlie came crawling along the ground, flat on their stomachs like moles. I asked John where he was going and his reply was "Christ! Mac, they've got a bead on us."

That was all too true, as the bullets from our own tanks, and the shells of the enemy caught us right in the middle of this crossfire. As we lay there, expecting to be filled with metal, I had this incredible vision of a sky just filled with little beings, with what looked like wings. Boy, did we need guardian angels. There was no sign of the lads from our second tank, and there was little doubt they had been burned alive. I did not feel like crawling into a trench. I looked towards the enemy area and saw to my horror six eight-wheeled armoured cars coming up the ridge at an angle and facing directly towards us as we lay there in the open, only about eighty yards away.

The desert is a most inhospitable place and the effort of crawling was bad enough at any time, but this was under fire. I remember Captain Thom whispering "Oh Mac, your backside's sticking up like a mountain." I resorted to pulling my body along the ground, trying not to make any dust as I went, when another hail of machine-gun bullets came at us. It's strange how solemn promises are made in times of adversity and crisis. Captain Thom said "Mac, if you're hit I won't leave you, and you won't leave me if I'm hit."

The enemy was so near, that I fully expected one of the armoured cars to approach and shoot us. It was incredible to think that only fifteen minutes after the advance had begun, we had been knocked out. We continued to drag our bodies along the ground, and a fresh burst of bullets smacked about us every few minutes. We just couldn't get away from the cars, and we were pretty demoralised by the heat and sand, as much as by the bullets. Shots skiffed my hair and I could actually smell the cordite. I would have cried if I had thought it might have helped, but we just dragged ourselves along, slipping into a trench at times to snatch a short rest. We could see a German officer standing on top of his armoured car watching us through binoculars. The Spanda machine-guns fired 1200 rounds per minute, and bullets continued to hit the ground around me, covering me with sand.

We had covered another agonising hundred yards or so away from the German armoured cars when an enemy tank came up on the flank about 200 yards or so from us. The officer gave bearings and levelled some accurate fire toward us. It was amazing that we could be shot at so many times and still survive. We had lost track of time as we continued our slow crawl, and the only thought in our minds was to survive somehow. I wondered if we should have found a trench like John and Charlie, but Thom's voice whispered out again "I hope they don't start shelling us, Mac."

We dragged our bodies along the ground in agony, waiting to be cut in half by enemy fire at any moment. We had been crawling for hours by now, and we had had enough, and decided to try to make a run for it. I wasn't sure whether I could even walk, let alone run, although we would certainly cover more ground. Apart from that, it was difficult to know when to run and when to dive for the ground again, as the German officer spotted us and opened fire, just missing me again. The first ray of hope came when we saw one of our tanks, and got to it before collapsing. The crew helped me up and I drank two quarts of water as their tank reversed about 100 yards. When I became aware of where I was, it was now 2.30 in the afternoon. My abundant dose of hell had lasted from 8.45 am until 2.00 in the afternoon - five hours of fear and pain which drained every ounce of strength from my tattered and torn body.

I headed for our replenishing vehicles and passed by a battery of 25-pounders. The crews noticed I was a bit of a mess, but all I could do was ask for a drink - polishing off three mugs of tea before continuing on my way. Ironically, the gun-crews said it had been a quiet morning. They couldn't fire any shells at the enemy, because there was so little space between the Germans and the tank crews who had bailed out and were lying on the ground, so near the enemy lines. Captain Thom was on another tank while I arrived at Padre Duthie's lorry. I must have looked a sorry sight, with no skin on my arms and knees, and pouring blood. My overalls were torn to shreds, and with a growth of fourteen days on my face I was not a pretty sight at all. Padre Duthie opened a tin of peaches and poured a generous ration of milk. All I could think of then was to bed down and sleep, although I had no equipment with me apart from my service revolver.

As night approached, some of the lads gave me a couple

of blankets, and I no sooner lain down than I was fast asleep -
only to be rudely awakened, as nervous spasms actually
seemed to lift my entire body right off the ground, so that I hit
my head on the axle of the lorry I was under. Then, shortly
after midnight, the officer commanding our squadron and
Captain Foster, our second-in-command, came looking for me.
They shook hands and congratulated me on my 'courageous
escape', so it was obvious they had been speaking to Captain
Thom. Next morning, I was issued with fresh kit for the second
time, and wandered across to ask the cook if I could have a
little water to shave off my fortnight's growth. Sarcastically,
he suggested I bring my water bottle accross, but I told him I
no longer had one, and had only the clothes I was wearing. I
suppose being twenty miles behind the lines gave no concept
of what it was like at the front, so perhaps I was asking too
much.

As I wandered aimlessly around, I met the commander
from the first of our troop tanks to be knocked out. He looked
at me, borrowed a truck, and told me he was taking me to the
doctor. The orderly had one look at me and sent for the medical officer. "Laddie," he said, "you're in a right mess, and
you're going to need a bit of treatment." Eventually I emerged,
heavily bandaged arms and legs making any kind of movement
difficult. When I tried to go to sleep that night, I found I
couldn't get my body down on the ground, and I needed some
of the lads to hold me until I hit the ground. Once down, I
couldn't get up without help, and this lasted for a few weeks.
Captain Thom had a daily chat with me, and seemed most
anxious that I should go with him wherever he went, but I told
him I wasn't nearly ready for another tank.

While we were thus separated, the Knightsbridge attack
continued, during which so many tanks were lost. When
Captain Benzie from Milltimber was killed, Captain Thom
took command of his squadron, and was shot out of two tanks.
Another tank was shipped for him and while he was standing
outside it a shell landed nearby and he was killed by shrapnel.

So we lost a very special man who could never be replaced and who had been due for a bravery award with others of our crew.

It was some days before we met up with Charlie, our operator, and John the gunner. They had stayed in the trench instead of crawling. They had remained there until sundown and then, by the aid of the North Star, they began walking eastwards. They walked all night and when they came across any vehicles, they had to approach carefully to check whether they were enemy or friendly, for obvious reasons. As first light was breaking, they came across some vehicles and by now had decided to approach, whether it was the enemy or not, so low had their morale become. When they were challenged by the guards - in English - they knew they were safe at last.

CHAPTER NINE

Stemming the German Tide

THREE WEEKS later I was astounded to be called back to the tanks in spite of my injuries. I had to get someone to roll my blankets, and pack my kit, before I struggled to even climb on to the lorry. When we arrived at our destination, the officer in charge asked me what I was supposed to do, in my state, and I simply had to say that I had been detailed. He promised me that he wouldn't use me unless he absolutely had to, that the tanks we were to take over were still fortunately in action, and change-overs were not considered wise at this time.

We were loaded on to the lorry once more, and boy was I glad. The Germans had knocked out a large number of our tanks, and were on the advance. We retreated by lorry for days until we reached Mersa Matrij and this gave me ample time to complete my healing. Another few days and the call came again. I was given another American Honey, and I shook like a leaf as I sat once more in the driver's seat, wondering what on earth was keeping me going.

The German advance continued miles each day and as we retreated we came through Tobruk where the lads were working away as if nothing was happening. By nightfall, Tobruk had fallen and hundreds had been taken prisoner, including those we had so recently passed. The tanks we took

over at Mersa Matrij had previously been manned by For-
farshire Yeomanry who had never been in action. A rather
cruel twist of fate? We took the tanks west, as the German
advance continued eastwards, and by nightfall they had taken
the town.

We were now, however, behind the German advance and
our role was to harry their progress with our meagre fourteen
tanks. It was a very uncomfortable period, and orders came that
no-one should sleep alongside, or outside the tanks. The drivers
were ordered to sleep in their seats, with the rest of the crew
either in the tank, or underneath it. I don't know who was
being harrassed, as we were continually attacked by tanks,
infantry and shell-fire. There were daily skirmishes, and no-
one seemed to know where the enemy was at any one time.

We woke one morning to find ourselves surrounded by
Italian lorries, guns and infantry. We were in action before first
light, and an enemy shell exploded five yards from our tank,
forcing us to change position before the gunner could adjust his
range. We launched a full scale attack, and it was our turn to be
on top, as their infantry ran wildly about trying to get on to any
vehicle. Some didn't make it, and we destroyed all their
transport vehicles which they had been forced to abandon.

We headed south that day, and were just about to settle
for the night, when shells and machine-gun bullets smacked all
around us. Few slept that night, with three of the four crews
standing guard, though some were asleep on their feet. With
daily action, no food and little sleep, we could hardly keep our
eyes open. There was tension the following day, for we were to
leave at nightfall for an all-night drive through enemy lines,
back to our own forces. Orders were issued that no-one could
sleep, as we would be passing enemy tanks all night, and had to
keep on the move. I'll never forget that night. We moved in
line-ahead and if I lost the tank in front, we had to drive
through clouds of dust. I remember one occasion, when all the
crew were asleep except me, since someone had to drive the
tank. In the middle of the night, when I was trying to keep my

eyes open, Lieutenant Manby woke up with a start. He kicked
the radio operator and asked if he had received the last message. More than a little puzzled, the operator said that he had
not, to which Manby replied "It's all right. I was just making
sure you were awake."

The gunner was rolled up like a ball at the bottom of the
tank, and there were hairy moments when I found myself
nodding off for a few seconds. There came a moment of panic
when the commanding officer came on air, to roar at the
navigator "For Christ's sake get a move on! Don't you see
those German tanks to our right?" I looked out myself and saw
clearly that there were outlines of about twenty of the brutes.
By daylight though, we had made contact with our own forces,
who were forming the Alamein line between the sea and the
Qatara Depression. It was the narrowest part of the desert we
could hold against the Germans. We had been promised some
rest when we got back to our lines, but promises are often
made to be broken, and by that afternoon we were in action.

A force of twenty-five German tanks was advancing
toward our forces, so we formed a battle line to make an attack
on them. Our shells, however, simply bounced off their tanks,
since the Honey's gun was .37 solid shot but with no real
penetrating power. As they passed through our battle line we
closed formation and had better success attacking their vehicles
at the rear. When they turned back on us, though, that was a
whole new proposition. A tank close to us was hit and set on
fire, and two of the crew were seen to be standing in the middle
of the desert, completely dazed, with hardly any skin on their
bodies. We made to pick them up, but another tank was in a
better position. Again the night brought no sleep, our tank
being required to tow some 25-pounder guns off soft sand
where they had been stuck.

There were only twelve serviceable tanks left now, which
in itself was not exactly a viable force, but we were
nevertheless taken to the H.Q. of the 7th Armoured Division.
The object was to form a mobile force to harass the Germans

once again, being comprised of our tanks, along with a company of infantry and a battery of 25-pounder guns. The 'Powers that Control' had a job and a half for us that night. The officer said that we had an attack but he felt we were in no fit state to do anything. He reckoned he had never seen men in such a state and that we must rest and recover.

That was right, for I didn't have strength even to stop the tank, far less go into battle once more. When I asked to see a doctor, he asked me what food I'd had, to which I replied that I'd had none at all. When he discovered that I hadn't had any sleep either, he arranged for me to be held in the ambulance for some days, and to receive extra food. I reached the ambulance that evening, fell asleep and slept for some 36 hours. With that rest and decent food, I soon felt so much better.

Before I was able to rejoin my crew there was an attack which killed two of our most able sergeants. I had such admiration for these Regulars, and there was no way we reinforcements to the 1st R.T.R. could ever have matched up to their professionalism and efficiency. I was glad to be back with my tank, not that I was all that brave, but there was a funny inner feeling of *doing one's bit*. "Why should I hold back," I used to think, "and let someone else have all the aggro?"

I always remembered Captain Thom's words after one of our life or death sorties - "I don't mind dying, McGregor" to which I replied "Aye, sir, but I don't want to die." I thought about him now, just as I thought about those poor lads from the tank who must have been burned alive. Had the shells hit 12 inches nearer, our petrol tank would have gone up, and that would have been the end of us. You know, I've seen a tank hit, and for that one awful moment you think nothing's happened, when suddenly there's a cloud of black smoke and a mass of flames, a truly fearsome and blood-chilling sight to behold.

I look back often, and wonder how we faced death day after day, with no sleep or food, pushing our bodies to the limit and beyond, both physically and mentally. We never ceased to be surprised each evening that we were actually still alive.

After the two sergeants were killed, replacements were found as usual, though not with the same efficiency. As a corporal I was quite likely to be asked at any given moment to take command of a tank, and indeed there was at this time one corporal in command of a troop of tanks.

This flying column which we had joined, with eight 25-pounder guns and infantry, made many sorties but were excluded from one in particular. It was a mission left to our 12 tanks, to round the Quatara depression and attempt to shoot up some German transport vehicles. There had never been an attempt before, to cut through the depression, and little wonder. What looked like normal sand surface, sank some 10 inches under the weight of our tanks. We covered twenty miles and were nearly wiped out.

To escape the sinking, we went up the escarpment to high ground, but the vehicles had moved, and we had to make our way back again. I had used twenty gallons of petrol to cover the twenty miles, and I had only twenty gallons to get us back. The Germans had pulled their guns down to block our way, and getting off that escarpment was a terrifying business. We had to come down a slope which was almost perpendicular, and we were terrified of toppling over and being at the mercy of the guns. We made it, but there had been too many anxious moments, and we realised now, why the defence line at El Alamein was anchored on the Quatara depression. There was no hope of any force using the ground we had just experienced to make an attack.

We too continued our sorties to harass the Germans, and as we began, things were not quite so hectic. Now it was a holding operation as the German advance was halted. But we heard that before the defence line was properly secured, H.Q. in Cairo was burning papers. Gunfire could be heard in Cairo, but now that our building of the line was complete, we could enjoy some rest.

CHAPTER TEN

Tripoli Times

IT WAS some change to be able to enjoy a few brews each day. Our staple food was corned beef, although there were many days and weeks when we got virtually no food at all. There were no vegetables or fruit, and if it wasn't corned beef it was tinned meat - never quite what mother would have made.

We had set out from Cairo in the month of May, and it was now the last days of July, and I was alive. We were soon refitted with a new set of tanks, and I had another American Honey for the next attack. We had gone beyond trying to think what might come next, and just accepted what was to be our lot. We simply tried to hold on to what was most precious to us - our lives. That, let's face it, was all we could do.

One day a message came round about a padre service at the H.Q. tank, and about sixty lads attended. It was very informal as the padre spoke about Captain Scott's mission to the South Pole. He had just been emphasising Scott's lack of fear amidst such dangers when a German 109 fighter flew across our tanks. There was always a rush to see who got to the ack-ack guns first, and soon all the tank guns were blazing away at the enemy aircraft, but he got away. When the gunfire subsided, the padre dragged himself from under the tank saying: "Is he away yet?"

We were holding the southern sector of the line, and there was a lot of movement in the area. Patrols had to be active, but the job of probing the enemy lines after dark was left to the poor infantry lads. Life was never pleasant in the desert, and it was impossible to drink a cup of tea without finding flies stuck around the mug even while we were drinking. When we were cooking, the flies would be round the pan while it was still on the stove. Out of the action we could vary our food a little, and we tried our hand at steam pudding according to our desert recipe:

'Put some biscuits in a bag recovered from a German tank;

Smash on a tank until crushed like meal;

Stir in some margarine and - on rare occasions -

Add a few raisins to make a fruit sponge;

Steam for a few hours.'

On those few occasions when we were issued with boiled sweets and a little chocolate, I would melt the chocolate with some flour making a sauce. So now we had 'steamed fruit pudding with chocolate sauce'. It was sometimes said within the squadron "It's good to be on Mac's tank - he can cook." Other times I would use the tins of meat and vegetables with ground biscuits to produce 'meat patties and veg'. I know how the poor housewife must feel, having spent hours preparing the meal, only for it to be devoured in minutes. However it passed the day.

It was quite amusing and informative, when out of action, to see what we could do with the contents of our food lockers. There was one amusing incident when we built an oven with an oil drum and, with a mug of flour, margarine and Andrews salts for raising I tried my hand at puff pastry. I rolled the margarine and flour on a copy of the *Tripoli Times*, only to find that my baking now carried all the latest news. I kneaded the mixture over and over again hoping it would rise to an inch of pastry, but it came out more like a shortbread. So we raided a German depot and found lemon squash which I boiled with margarine to make lemon curd. I had some marshmallows and so I gave my shortbread base a lemon curd and marshmallow topping. It was the highlight of the day, and everyone was raving about 'Mac's baking'. This was certainly one of our better days.

The period between establishing the El-Alamein line and the preparations for the big push was termed 'stalemate', but it was anything but stalemate for the poor infantry. They had to maintain constant touch with the enemy to see what was happening. The British were laying mines, and no doubt Jerrie was doing the same, and massive supplies of new equipment were arriving. Strangely enough, we didn't dwell too much on past losses during this waiting time, or about what might happen in the next blitz. Air activity was constant, and the ack-ack guns on our tanks were always at the ready. Ideas that we were to be given four days leave before the big day proved right, and we spent them at the Union Jack Club in Cairo.

It was so good to be in Cairo, where anything could be purchased, and where there was always an abundancy of water in the form of showers. The regimental doctor told me, before I left, to get plenty of eggs since my blood was in a shocking state. No wonder. It was easy enough to peel skin from the hands, and allow the poison to seep away, but it was another thing for the hands to heal. Many a time I had lumps beneath my arms which were worrying enough, and my health was precarious to say the least.

Nevertheless the days seemed to pass, even if there was little to do and no contact with anyone other than the lads of the squadron. We stayed within sight of our tanks at all times, for there was never a moment when you could say that you weren't needed. I think we all felt that death was inevitable, but what form it might take was what tended to nip the brain. For me, it was the dread of being burned alive in the tank, which I felt would be a long and terrible way to die.

We knew the big day was fast approaching, and even more so when a regimental church service was held - not a frequent occurrence. It was telling that they took the risk of gathering about two hundred men in such a small area. I remember vividly the fact that Padre Duthie had fairly big lips, and that the flies swarmed around them, no matter how hard he tried to get rid of them. I felt very uneasy about this service as if it were a benediction for those about to die. It was certain that before victory was won in North Africa, many of us would be required to make the ultimate sacrifice.

Certainly the massive accumulation of armour in our area suggested that an attack was imminent, and patrols by tanks and infantry were increasing. All around us anti-tank gunners were digging in, so well entrenched that their gun barrels were no more than eighteen inches above the ground. I remember thinking that if an offensive was indeed successful, there was no way the lads could escape, dug in as they were.

The Germans attacked, and we were waiting for them in prepared defensive positions. The anti-tank gunners and our tanks waited until the enemy tanks were two to three hundred yards from us before opening up. Nearly all their tanks were knocked out, and it appeared to us that at last we had given the enemy something to really think about and regret.

This success seemed to settle our line, and we knew that another attack like this was rather unlikely. We completed our plans for an attack on the German lines spearheaded by an artillery attack which would last one and a half hours. The night of October 23rd found us packing up during the early evening as the advance on the enemy began.

I well recall an incident on the way when we stopped in the desert for a short time. We dug a hole and placed a couple of petrol cans at the bottom for a make-shift latrine. The tank commanders were usually on the wireless when moving to the front, but there was a momentary lapse. One commander used his microphone to warn: "Watch that shit-hole, Jock, or we'll stink for a month." The commanding officer's operator came on the air "Get on I.C." How could we fail to grasp at a little humour when faced with those ominous clouds ahead? Zero hour for the artillery barrage to begin was 10.30 pm, and dead on time the sky was lit up with flashes. The whole Front, from the sea to the Qatara depression seemed ablaze, and we might even have enjoyed the spectacle, had we not known just what it was and what it meant.

We quickly advanced to our minefields, in front of which Jerry had laid his own. Our tanks were in line-ahead and led by the squadron commander, Gus Holliman, who had once been a member of the Long Range Desert Group. He was in just the same mould as Captain Thom in terms of bravery and daring. So we were sitting before Jerry's first minefield, and the feeling cannot really be truly described. It was terrifying as we sat in the middle of a complete ring of fire with shells, anti-tank shells, bullets and bombs raining in on us from every direction. Surely there was nothing which could ever survive such an assault, and I was shaking with fear.

I was sitting in the tank with the engine running, when a young infantryman came up and shouted to me. As I removed my earphones, he called "What about the machine guns in front of that ridge?" He was obviously petrified with fear as well, but I could offer little more than cold comfort: "If you look after the anti-tank guns, we'll look after the machine-gunners."

I got the feeling the lad had a premonition that his number was up, but that was a feeling we all knew at times. It was 12.30 am and should have been dark but for the gunfire which created a false daylight. We had to accompany the infantry into the minefield and the lead tank suddenly got the order to advance. Again the squadron commander led by example, rather than detail others, and two more tanks followed. In no time at all, news came back that two of the three had been knocked out, and our tank was next in line.

The troop commander ordered us to conform to him, and the Royal Engineers were supposed to go ahead and clear a path for us. The moment I touched the starter and booster switch, I knew that I would never start that tank again. It was a strange feeling, but we made our way in behind the commander's tank as a tracer anti-tank shell landed just beside him. I slowed down and Bungy Whiteland, my commander, said "Mac, did you see that?"

I sped past, and the next moment a terrific explosion left us leaning to one side, with the inside of our tank filled with so much dust that we could hardly see one another. I wasn't sure what had happened, but with the tank leaning over, I couldn't feel my legs or feet. I opened the flaps and as I tried to get out, I put my hands down to make sure my legs were still attached to my body. I didn't know what had happened, although I reckoned we had hit a mine and that the bottom of the tank must have been ripped away, allowing all that dust inside.

Before the attack began, we were told that if our tank was knocked out we should use it as a pillbox, but that was one order we did *not* obey. With all the crew safely out, we were surrounded by flying metal and doubtful about our chances of survival. As we stood there, another tank came back down the line and picked us up. There was such intense firing that the four of us clung on to a piece of metal less than half an inch thick, trying to avoid the machine-gun fire. I don't know how we hung on, but the instinct for self-preservation was strong. We were taken back about a hundred yards before we started running. When we came to the commanding officer's tank, Bungy climbed on top, gave his call sign, and said "We've been knocked out".

The commanding officer told us to "Get the hell out of here! You're out of action." Blunt but fair, given the tense situation we were in. We walked about a mile, and daylight was breaking as we reached our forward replenishing vehicle, having lost all our kit for the *third* time. The cook lorry was there and we asked if we could have some tea, only to be asked once more where our mugs were. We said that they were in our tank in the middle of a Jerry minefield, so we had to go into a hole to get an empty milk tin from which to drink our tea. What kindly folk, eh?

We got transport to return to our rear replenishing vehicle, where we were issued with fresh kit before enjoying relative peace and calm to catch a night's sleep. Charlie, who was our radio operator when we had to bail out of our tank at Knightsbridge, was again in our crew. Would a third time be lucky? The next day, a leisurely breakfast was followed by the call for Sergeant Whiteland and Corporal McGregor to prepare to go up to the tanks. Hardly possible, you might think, but true all the same. By nightfall we were back among the tanks. The squadron commander appointed Whiteland to our tank and then said to me "Sergeant Whiteland, take over that tank there. McGregor, I don't know what I'm going to do with you, but you're far too precious not to be in the tanks."

A Sergeant Jones, when he knew I was spare, came to me and asked me to come on to his tank. I didn't volunteer, but he asked his sqaudron commander who said that would be fine if Mac agreed. I asked Jones what was wrong with his driver, and he replied "He keeps stalling the engine, and he's going to get us all killed."

With my kit packed, I transferred to his tank, and by the next day we were once more in the middle of it. We were trying to penetrate Jerry's defences, and getting a pretty hot time of it. When we were held up by four anti-tank guns, the squadron commander asked for a troop of tanks with 75mm high-explosive shells to clear our path. "You have the vehicles there - use them."

Our troop was nearest their guns, and our troop commander didn't like being delayed, so he replied that he would see what he could do. Our three-tank troop advanced slowly toward their guns, with our machine-guns blasting away. We were in battle line with about 20 to 30 yards between each tank. All at once, Jones shouted down the intercom "STOP FIRING! ADAVANCE RIGHT AS FAST AS YOU CAN!"

As I turned, three of the lads from another tank were jumping up and down by the side of their tank which had taken a hit from anti-tank fire. Their commander had been killed, and I pulled up as near the lads as I could, so that they were able to jump up on to the front of our tank. I couldn't see a hole in the side of the tank facing us, so I drew up alongside, to give our tank as much cover as possible. I reckoned if I moved past it, we'd catch it too, since all it needed was the same range. When we did move, I expected any moment to be hit, so I took swerving action to make it as difficult as possible. I had to stop twice, as the constant swerving made it difficult for the chaps on the front to keep a hold, even though their lives depended on it.

We took them back about five hundred yards until we hit a patch of safe ground, and then I realised what a poor lot they were, with chunks out of their bodies. We used up all our field dressings, and every bandage we had, but we just couldn't stop the bleeding, whilst the flies were all over them. We sent for the ambulance, which took them off, and then we got back to the fray again with not a lot of confidence.

We joined the one other survivor of our troop and shared many hazardous days. As the Germans gradually lost hold of their territory, we were flooded with hundreds of Italian prisoners. Our crew took a chance and went out to disarm as many of them as possible, using signs rather than words, for obvious reasons. We did manage to get them to discard their equipment and revolvers, putting as much as possible in our tank, and then discarding all but the revolvers, which we held on to. I remember at one point, having about 40 revolvers lying on the floor of the tank, nice neat Berettas which we had no difficulty in giving away.

With that little side taken care of, we went back into action with a different kettle of fish - the Germans. We captured a German anti-tank gun with a crew of ten, when their transport broke down and left them stranded. Since we were the leading tanks, we had no one to take them off our hands so we lined them up on a bank of sand near their gun. I went up to the ack-ack gun and fired a burst of bullets into the ground near to where they stood. I then told them to line up where I had fired, and the look on their faces told me they didn't know what to expect. It was really an act of bravado on my part to dissuade them from any attempt to escape. We left them with the food rations they had and took their Lugar revolvers. It took some time for our infantry to arrive and escort them back to the prisoner-of-war camps. Now it was back to the front line to join the other tanks of our troop.

We were advancing, but the battle was far from one-sided, and both sides had heavy tank losses. During a lull, when our forces got a bit mixed up, I chatted to the tank crews of another unit. I asked them about Harold, one of the lads who'd been called up with us, and who I believed had been placed in their unit. I was told, to my great sadness, that he had just been killed. Again I wondered just what the next blow would be. Nightfall brought brief respite, and I had time to think about the advance now in progress. With such large numbers of casualties behind us, we were lucky to be alive at all.

The brunt of the advance in our sector was being borne by the 7th Armoured Division (The Desert Rats), the 1st and 5th Royal Tank Regiments and the 4th County of London Yeomanry. These were the vanguard of the advance as we made several miles each day, in face of sporadic resistance which made life difficult. As we advanced next day, there was another almighty bang and crunch as the tank hit another mine and swerved crazily. We were in the middle of a minefield, with both tracks in a heap, and the sides of the tank torn apart. We were very much on our own, and even the box with our emergency rations had been shot off the previous night, so we were left with just the food in our locker.

Other tanks suffered the same fate and were evacuated, but it was a bit demoralising being on our own as we waited for the salvage vehicle. We had some tea, very little milk and no sugar, until we managed to 'rescue' some boiled sweets from a lorry and crush them to sweeten our brew. Funny, we might have been well pleased to enjoy the few days of relative peace, but there was a war to be won, and we were sitting it out.

At last the recovery vehicle arrived and transported us to our unit, only for us to find out that our regiment was out of action. It had lost so many tanks as to become ineffective, and was awaiting new vehicles. The fresh tanks soon arrived - Shermans - with 75mm guns and machine-guns, and our squadron got British Cromwells with 6-pounder guns. These tanks were fairly lightly armoured at about one and a half to two inches in thickness, and needed so much more maintenance than the American tanks.

An American Sherman Tank

We were far behind the Front, and we had our tanks put on mobile transporters. It took us days on the move as we headed for the Front again, but on the way we had a good deal. Our convoy of eighteen squadron tanks and carriers was stopped by the side of a road which ran east to west near the coast. As we stopped, we saw a group of about fourteen natives, one of whom carried a basket full of long loaves. We understood by sign language that they wanted a lift to Holmes. More in fun than necessity, I bargained with them to take them to Holmes for a loaf for each person. We agreed that those who were muskeen (without money) could pay later, and we transported the fourteen, sharing fourteen loaves with the transport drivers. When we stopped for the night, Gus Holliman, who was fluent in Arabic, marvelled at how we, with our few Arabic words, could do a deal which he couldn't, even with his language skills. Well we reckoned that, whatever, it *was* a good deal.

These lighter incidents were all too few, but it stopped us having our hearts in our boots all the time. Soon we had gone as far as we could by transport, and we felt a little envious of our transport drivers who could just turn around and go back, while we had to head for the hot zone. We didn't think too much about those who were non-combatant, for we were where we were, and we had to get on with it.

We formed battle line and drove toward Tripoli, which soon fell to our forces as Jerry retreated. A lull, for a day or so, meant that we had to clean our tanks and equipment with sand, although we considered this to be so much bullshit in the middle of a war. However, we soon learned the purpose of this, as Winston Churchill was coming to Tripoli to inspect the troops. I must confess that I wasn't too thrilled at all this paraphernalia, for someone who hardly saw us. This was borne out the next day when we lined up for revue beside our tanks, while Churchill passed by on a lorry.

The next day, it was back to the battle line again, and we had a pretty sticky time at Medineen. After having had a nasty time, as shells dropped uncomfortably close, we had a petrol blockage on the tank. We could hardly sit there and do nothing about it, so it was my job to get things sorted out. Being afternoon, and the tank engine having been running since 4.30 in the morning, a lot of heat had been generated. It was not the easiest business, to lie on top of an engine, reaching down the side of it to unlock the screws and get the carburretor bowl out, with sweat dripping all the time on to the engine. I had it almost off when Jerry started shelling again. The rest of the crew were safely inside the tank, but pouring sweat and with shrapnel flying all around, what could I do but hope - yes - hope? Thankfully, I got the stoppage cleared and got back inside, thinking how much life depended on a wee bit of luck.

Did I mention prayer? Yes, we all prayed in our own ways constantly, but I always wondered how some of our lads were chosen to make the supreme sacrifice. As our tanks became depleted, along with so many of our boys, I often pondered the possibility of survival. We had to lose 25 to 30 percent of our men before we were declared ineffective and re-equipped up to full crew strength, only to be depleted again.

Around this time, the 1st Army landed in Tunisia, and after quite some time they had failed to take Tunis. The 4th Indian Division and the 7th Armoured Division were ordered to the 1st Army Front, and we too made our way by tank trans-porter. This took a few days, as we had to travel far south to avoid the fighting. We were many days on this mission, skirt-ing around the fighting forces to arrive at the 1st Army sector. On the way, we bargained with the natives for chickens and eggs, using our tea for barter. It was a good trade and provided us with a real banquet. I still remember boiling a hen one night at ten o'clock so that we could have cold chicken the next day.

About this time we were confronted by a new tank which Jerry was using, called the Tiger. It was a very heavy tank weighing about 60 tons and mounting an 88mm gun. This gun had terrorised tank crews for some time, being easily mounted on the ground, something like a 37mm anti-aircraft gun. This weapon's powers of penetration were greater than any other enemy gun we had encountered, and it would have gone through most of our tanks. These Tiger tanks had eight to ten inches of armour in front so that even our 17-pounder anti-tank shells would have been useless when fired at the front of such a tank. The 17-pounder which our gun fired was more than 18 inches long with about 14 pounds of cordite. When this shell was fired, the flash spread about 10 yards to each side of the tanks, and the radio operator inside the tank, whose job it was to load the shell into the gun, had to be quite strong. And he had to remember to hide his face and close his eyes against the flash when it was fired. The tanks which carried these 17-

pounder shells were only used when a target for them had been defined.

A German Tiger I on display in Horse Guard Parade, London

On our journey, we met some American Army lads who were frantic to get as many souvenirs as possible. They were paying in the region of £20 for an automatic, and we were quite sorry we had given away so many of the Italian Berettas - talk about throwing away a fortune. We reckoned that in future we would sell anything for the good of the crew as a whole, presuming we were alive.

Once again we took up position for the attack, zero hour being 4.30 am for the Gurkhas and 8.30 am for us. The Gurkhas were truly professional fighting men, and we had tremendous respect for them. I was always so grateful that the Indian regiments were on our side. In the next attack, they were incredible, going into action without any prior artillery barrage, and, as ever, using stealth as their greatest weapon. We were now on our start-line, waiting the signal to engage, when I spotted a dead German officer lying near our tank. I went out and had a look, seeing he had a pair of binoculars and a revolver on him. I was worried he might be booby-trapped, so I attached our mine wire to his waist, and drew the tank back some twenty yards in case of explosion. There was none as he rolled over, and the binoculars and revolver began our crew's booty fund.

Now came the serious stuff, as we spread out along the top of the hill. Suddenly a massive air assault hit us with shells and machine-gun fire, and Sergeant Shields from Glasgow, our tank commander roared down the intercom "STOP, MAC! STOP, MAC! WE'RE UNDER FIRE." Dutifully I applied brake pressure - and nothing hapenned. I frantically struggled with the steering sticks, and then saw to my horror that the air-brake pressure was zero. I grabbed the gear handle to engage a gear, and it broke off level with the top of the gear box. With no brakes and no steering, we were off down the hill at a rate of knots. On the incline, we gathered speed very quickly, and as I gazed out of my four by two inch slit, I saw another tank moving at the foot of the hill. By this time we were travelling at about 30 miles per hour, but the tank in front didn't realise we were out of control, and didn't clear a path for us.

We hit it at the front and moved it about ten yards, its driver thinking he had been hit by a shell. I can still see Les Allan's head poking out of the driver's flap. His earphones were broken, and there was blood from his head streaming down the sides of his face. I have no doubt had we hit them midships we would all have been killed. With the speed and impact we wouldn't have been worrying any more about any booty fund ever again.

It was no time before our repair team arrived, and saw that the tracks on both tanks had been smashed up. They had no alternative but to fix one and disable the other, so that within the day one tank was ready to go once more. Guess who was to be the driver? Yes, it had to be yours truly, and once again we were in the line of fire.

An amazing advance had been made, and arriving at the

outskirts of Tunis, we advanced slowly through the streets. The Germans occupying the town were caught completely by surprise, and couldn't believe that they were shortly to be prisoners. The infantry were with us, and they soon rounded up prisoners, one being our perfect picture of a real Nazi. When told to move, he did so at his own pace, and I remember one of our lads saying to the infantry "Dinna bother wi' him. Just stick your bayonet up his arse."

In battle conditions, people are not always themselves, and how on earth could they be? It wasn't our job to clear the town, as we had other fields to conquer, and there were still thousands of Germans to be dealt with. Keeping on the move during daylight hours, with short nightly breaks, it was the same procedure again at first light. We were on fairly high ground overlooking the road the Germans had to use, and although our 6-pounder guns couldn't reach them, the other two squadrons, with their 75mm guns firing high-explosive shells, could. This action was kept up for a few days, and I was surprised that we had not made a final attack on them.

During this time, one interesting attitude came to light from our commanding officer, who insisted that the leading tanks keep him informed of the situation as it developed. "I could possibly advance," he said, "and take prisoners, with the probable loss of only six tanks."

What a thought. That might mean endangering the lives of twenty four men of the six crews, to be added to the 13,000 lost at El Alamein. That would be more than 13,000 mothers' sons, and to me there was little worth in any mother losing a son.

In due course, we heard that masses of Germans were being captured, and this at last began the last chapter in the North African campaign. We had momentary relief, and it was bliss to put our blankets down on grassy ground after the hardships of the desert floor. Would you believe it, a few days later we were back in the sand, settling on the barren wastes about fifteen miles from Tripoli? After my first action as a gunner, I was driving up to this final battle after Tunis, and by now I had been made up to sergeant, so ending my driving days.

CHAPTER ELEVEN

The Invasion of Italy

IT WAS a tank commander's life for me, and I knew that the end of the war in Africa did not spell the end of active service. So much was still to be done, and we were unlikely to be left here while other forces did the job. Our tanks were taken away and we were settled in bivouacs and tents. After a week or so, two lads from each squadron were to be sent to Cairo on a driver-mechanic Instructor Course, and I was one selected from A-squadron. We were to fly from Castle Beniot aerodrome but the plane had a fault and we were taken to Tripoli to complete the journey by sea. I would not have chosen to fly to Cairo but I suppose it was just the same to be shot out of the air as get killed on the ground. A small ship took us to Alexandria and we were under escort before arriving at the Cairo barracks where the course was to be held. It was said that any soldier who did not attain 80 percent in General Principles would be sent back to his unit. The whole course was interesting, and the General Principles course took about three weeks, with all our lads attaining over 80 percent and looking forward to the rest of the work. One week later, all the 7th Armoured Division personnel were ordered to return to their units at once. We all knew what was up.

Now it was to be across the water. When we joined our unit we got the news - the 7th Armoured was in reserve for the invasion of Sicily. There were still no tanks when we got back, but this was soon rectified when we were equipped with American Sherman diesels, with their 75mm gun and machine-gun turret. The armour wasn't as thick as the infantry Matilda tanks but they were powered by two 8-cylinder 2-stroke engines.

A Sherman tank in Italy

The first thing on the agenda was to waterproof these 'babies' for this was to be a new experience, invading from the sea. Again we simply had to get on with it. It took weeks to have all the pieces of metal welded on to the tanks, and the massive scoup-like things seemed to tower above tanks which were already ten feet high. The main thing was to protect the engine while the tracks and front would just have to take it. With everything ready - ammunition racks filled, emergency food supplies, stretcher and so on - we were all set.

While this went on, Sicily was invaded and it seemed unlikely we would be required after all. We heard that tank-landing ships were in Tripoli harbour, quite surely to transport us across the Mediterranean. Behind me was Fort Cupuso,

Tobruk, Knightsbridge, the retreat to Mersa Matrij and the battle of El Alamein. Then there had been the dash to Tunis with the loss of five tanks and unending days of undisguised horror.

Yet I was still in one piece and for that I gave thanks with all my heart. I was always comforted by the vision of my grandmother, and I said my prayers each night with the photo of her, sitting with a bible in her hand, close by me at this time. Grandma had stayed close to us in the latter years of her life, and as a schoolboy I was expected to go to her wee house every night. As she was nearly blind, she liked me to read a chapter of the Bible each evening, and although the child in me would sometimes want to rebel, I did it and then sat with her for a wee while. Then I waited outside until she locked her door and then sat on the edge of her bed, when I knew she was settled for the night. Latterly, when she was very frail, she stayed with us and it was I who sat with her during her last hours. One early morning about 2 am, she stirred slightly and I moistened her lips with a little brandy and water using a feather. She asked who was there and I told her it was me, and she said "Oh my Duncan, God bless you." I have no doubt that Grandma's blessing kept me going safely to this day even when the odds I faced in war seemed overwhelming. Her influence has guided me through years of war and peace, and I am proud to admit just how close she has always been to me. That is why she was there as I prayed day and night during the war days, when so many thoughts filled our hearts and minds.

The next phase was to be different as we crossed the water to face an unknown foe on a new terrain. We loaded our tanks on to the landing craft, three abreast in five rows. We had to chain the tracks carefully in case any of the tanks moved during the voyage. We set off from Tripoli on a perfectly calm sea. It took some time to cross as we watched for periscopes which we reckoned would be easily spotted in such a calm water. There was the expected shelling, but we were more intent on how we would disembark.

All was soon revealed as the landing-craft simply faced land and kept going until they stuck. The doors opened, and the tanks had to make their way down the ramp into the sea until it seemed as if the water would come right over the top. So we landed at Salerno, and were at first unopposed which was some small blessing. When we stopped about a mile inshore, we found ourselves in the middle of a tomato field, a world away from the barren wastes we had been so used to. There were vines as well, bursting with ripe grapes, and apple orchards ready for harvesting. We slowly pushed inland, with little enemy reaction, and I had time to realise that I was now commander of my tank. It was not a duty I relished but that was the way of things. I remember one night we settled in an apple orchard in the midst of rain, and with our blankets soaking. I had the strangest dream that I was standing in the kitchen at home, with mother and father there. I had just said to them "I never thought someday I'd be standing here...." when suddenly a kick from the guard told me it was time to be up and at them.

What a terrible day I had, wondering what on earth my dream meant, or if it was some presentiment. However, I survived it, and the next day we moved forward for the attack. About 50 tanks rumbled up the road, and when we reached our destination, the cry went up "SWITCH OFF!" as if that made any difference, since the Germans must have heard us coming for miles. We were close to a vineyard with its cross-member poles heavy with grapes, and standing about the height of our tanks. Bob McGregor, our troop commander, said that our three tanks had a job to do that morning. We were just not accustomed yet to so much close country, which afforded cover for tanks and enemy guns, which we hadn't had in the desert.

As we moved forward, a shell burst inches away from Bob's tank and we had to move carefully. We captured an anti-tank gun crew and I had to guard them, sitting on the back of my tank, until the infantry came some time later. Believe me these infantry lads were in no mood to take prisoners since they'd had a rough time that morning, seeing many of their comrades killed. I don't know what happened to the Germans since we were more intent on what was happening around us.

Besides our troop, there were another four troops of tanks engaged at different places in the Front. It was terrifying listening to the wireless as one tank after another was knocked out at ranges from 50 to 100 yards. The Germans were obviously waiting for us after hearing our tanks the night before. Our troop was not engaged in this phase so we stayed where we were until nightfall. Next morning we counted the cost. Only five out of nineteen tanks survived. Sergeant Jones, our tank commander when we transported the three lads to safety after their tank was knocked out and the tank commander killed, was awarded the Military Medal. It's tragic to think that his was one of the fourteen tanks knocked out with the loss of all crew.

It was a lesson in tank misuse in terrain like this, and we were wary some days later as we pushed forward towards the River Gorigliano. We hit some sandy ground and lost a track. It couldn't possibly be refitted in soft sand like this, so we had to add an extra plate and change it back to normal size when we reached solid ground again. Back on the road, with another tank helping us, we were busily involved staying alive and mobile. Some 2000 yards away was an overlooking hill, and a shell came from this area without any warning. This was merely a 'ranger' shell, but soon others began to rain down on us thick and fast.

We received ten rounds of gunfire, which was ten shells from each of four guns. I heard one coming too close for comfort and dived into the doorway of a house standing near to our tanks. Out of the corner of my eye I saw one of our lads his body a few feet off the ground with the impact of a shell. We couldn't get near Da' Bell as we called him since he was over 30 years of age. By the time we did reach him he was dead, covered in blood and ripped to pieces by shrapnel. Two other lads were injured but not seriously, and our blankets had been

blown off the tanks and ripped to bits while the wireless set
was full of shrapnel. As if this wasn't bad enough, our gun
barrel had a large chunk blown out of it, so we reckoned that
we were lucky still to be alive.

We wrapped Da' Bell in some of the blanket material and
buried him beside the house. We had all liked him, and I made
a careful map reference of his grave since the Army was
always anxious to have as accurate a record as possible of
where its casualties were to be found. We had to summon
expert opinion for the damaged barrel. An officer told us to fire
a shot and see what happened. I suggested that he could be in
the tank when the shot was fired if he wanted. Eventually we
had to withdraw and have another turret fitted to our tank.

We were told that we were to be taken home for the
invasion of Europe and each day was an anguishing exercise of
staying alive until we could get home. After weeks of holding
the Line it was a joy to be ordered to pull back, although most
of us had to stand guard each night as Jerry came to within a
hundred yards or so to have a pot-shot. Still, guard duty was a
small price to pay for this momentary relief.

CHAPTER TWELVE

Home for D-Day

HANDING OVER our tanks was a huge relief, especially as we were hoping to see home again. After a few weeks we were boarding the Cameronia at Naples for the voyage home. It was with great joy and a good deal of longing that we sailed past Gibralter and headed north toward the white cliffs of Dover. On 4th January 1944, just three years and a few days since we left Liverpool, we docked at Glasgow. We had been away a long time, and the lads crowded to one side of the ship as we docked, just to see our homeland. Although we were soon on our way to camp in England, it was still the same island, and before long I was en route to Aberdeen for home leave.

I didn't mention that on my embarkation leave I had married Ina although we had had so little time together. It was good to be re-united. Letters from home were always such an uplift when our spirits were low. As the train left Stonehaven, I was filled with a terrible fear - I don't know why - but everything seemed to settle down when I saw Ina and my folks at home. But how could all be settled when we virtually had to start all over again?

The effects of these past years had taken their toll, and there was just that something which was difficult to pinpoint. Around Kinmuck, it was as if life was going on just as it had when the world had been at peace, and the tranquility was like a balm. Most of the young lads were exempted because of their work, and although I didn't expect a hero's welcome, very few were aware at all of what was happening in the world. Maybe it was a good thing too, and I enjoyed the sufficiency of food, with only a few things unavailable.

As you would expect, the leave days passed quickly, and it was back to camp where the routine was quickly re-established. Before long, two driving and maintenance instructors from each squadron were sent to a course at Borington, the tank school. The tutors were very good to us, though they felt at times we were overpowering, which was not the case since we had no experience of the tanks with which we were to be issued.

One instructor told us "Don't think because you've been abroad in action you know it all. There is always something we can teach you, and every tank has its own peculiarities." He told us that we would learn how to take a tank over a ten foot hole, and we looked forward to this, not really believing it was possible. In fact, we didn't see this demonstration, but we had the opportunity of seeing every detail of the tanks we would be using. There were cut-parts of every section of the engine - Rolls Royce - in two 8-cylinder banks. The armour was only one to two inches thick, while the armaments were a 6-pounder gun and a Besa machine-gun. Back at camp, I submitted an application for interview with the commanding officer of our squadron. I made my case that I was incapable of facing another phase of the war, to which he replied "With your experience, you are irreplaceable."

I doubted that very much, for it was only sheer ignorance that enabled me to face my first few actions, while experience only served to make me frighteningly aware of what might happen to me. I felt that fresh blood should be used, and I knew that we were going to face another dose of the same all over again. Units taking part in the Invasion had landing times, and we were D-Day plus one.

The first sign of something happening was when we were

transported to London and sealed in one of the football stadiums. I mean sealed, for only those who were bringing in essential rations were allowed in or out. Day after day as we waited, the 6.30 am news was eagerly awaited, until we were at length taken from the stadium to board ship. We had known it would not be long, and the 6.30 news on the morning of June 6th said it all: "German news agencies reported today a landing of troops on the coast of France. British sources have not confirmed this."

Things were really happening now, with the movement of ships by the dozen, and planes which had all been painted black with white stripes for easy identification. We moved slowly across the water away from the white cliffs, with hope that things would not be quite as bad as we pictured. It was not, however, going to be easy, even after such a long period of preparation.

Among tank crews we seldom related what had occurred during the day, since it was just part of what was expected of us as the defenders of a free world. What was the spirit and

A Cromwell tank in France

means which kept us going from one battle to the next? I'm pretty sure it was the desire to do anything which would protect our precious families and homes, and that seemed worthwhile no matter what the cost might be. None of us wanted to die, but the possibility was never far from our minds, surrounded as we were by terrible uncertainties. As I strolled round the tanks at night on guard duty, I would gaze up at the sky and think that the same sky was being seen by those at home. Yet the few thousand miles between us still made for a feeling of remoteness and hopelessness.

I should like, at this point, to quote a wee prayer which seemed to sum up my thoughts and hopes during those terrible times:

"Oh Father, go with us through the demands of another day;
Protect us, if it be Your Will, and may we not be burned alive.
Do not preserve my life at the cost of any of my pals.
I accept what You have in mind for me, so take from me what You need,
And may we do Your Will"

I imagined the landing force to be like Dunkirk in reverse, with all sorts of ships - large and small, battle-ships, landing craft and destroyers. D-day plus one passed and we were still not ashore, which didn't really surprise us. It must have been so difficult to have everything go to plan, and when we did get ashore there was so much to do. At least we had a foothold on the continent and with such massive forces to come, success was never really in any great doubt.

It was action almost immediately, with the Panzer divisions there in fairly large numbers, although with such a broad coastline there could be no real defence in depth.

Opposite Oaen was the battlefield, and day after day it was like coming up against a brick wall. This offensive lasted some two to three weeks until, according to Intelligence, we were faced with eight to nine German divisions. Losses were expected, and came, but the strategy was good and was to pay off, as our sector attacked and attacked again until the enemy forces became concentrated. This left the end of their line barely defended, and this was the chance for Paton's American forces to launch an offensive and make many miles during the next days. That broke the defensive line and opened up the whole area of France to the east. Enemy contact was ferocious, but every day was another we survived in one piece, however unpleasant the action was.

A German Panzer IV tank

The close country, as we called it, after the open desert was always very dangerous. We had a troop of tanks on a road crossing all night, and in the morning I, as senior sergeant, had to lead up this road. At the junction, the officer in charge told me that the Germans had been moving guns and tanks all through the night, so I told the gunner to take the armour-piercing shell out of the breach and replace it with high-explosive shell. I also instructed our gunner John - who had been the gunner on that unpleasant incident when our tank was set on fire at Knightsbridge - that if he saw anything move he should let go at it, since it was all enemy ahead. As soon as I said that, John's nerve broke, and he was trying to push past me, shouting: "Oh Duncan, I can't fire this gun. Let me out! Let me out!" I spoke quietly to him, and assured him that I wouldn't go round a corner or past a junction without first 'sussing' it out on foot. So at each opening and corner, I first took a walk from the tank, and in all honesty there was that part of me which hoped that someone would shoot me and put an end to this hell. I felt as if I was slowly becoming paralysed and I kept telling Johnny if he saw anything while I was out of the tank he should get an estimated range and fire. If I copped it, he was to take the tank back out of immediate danger.

It was more than three years now since my first action at Fort Capuso, and I really wondered how the body could take all this strain without completely giving in. Again we survived the day. I wanted to see the doctor but this was not possible, so it was into another nasty position a few days later. Our troop of three tanks was sent forward to hold the line, and the officer commanding our troop stationed two tanks within 50 yards of one another; my tank was sent forward 200 yards on its own. The enemy was all around, and our two rear tanks could observe but be of no practical use.

I put my tank into a corner near a hedge and against the trees, before taking a seat on the back to keep watch on the rear, and asking Johnny to look toward the front. We had been there since first light, and had not seen any Germans, until the early evening, when a glance to the front gave me the shock of my life. About 20 yards away, a German was lying on his side watching us through binoculars, and at that range he must have known the colour of my eyes. I shouted to Johnny and reversed from our enclosed position, with the trees on my right and the hedge in front. I reversed to hull down - that was having the tank half hidden to fire the gun without danger to ourselves. I couldn't believe that this was anything but a German patrol, and that they had had cover to reach within a few yards of us. I pictured one with a phosphorous grenade having a go at us and setting fire to the tank. However we saw no infantry, and when we assembled that night, I was made to look a coward by the second-in-command of our squadron: "That'll make nice reading in some German's diary tonight, " he moaned, "British tank retreats from one infantryman."

Obviously everyone was confused about the right position, and our troop officer was not about to offer any comfort. A few weeks later, I was relieved from my tank and put in reserve, since I was obviously not daring enough. That was a pretty fair assessment, and it wasn't exactly heart rending to be out of the tanks. If they thought that was punishment, then who was I to contradict them?

CHAPTER THIRTEEN

Into the Depths

WITHIN ABOUT six weeks, I was transferred to a forward tank delivery unit which suited me fine, and after a month or so there, a clerk came round asking for our demob numbers. I told him mine was 28 and asked what this was for, only to be told that 28 and under could be sent to the Far East. With my luck, I reckoned I would be parcelled off there next morning.

I reported sick and told the doctor my state of mind and body. He told me to wait until the parade was over, and then he sat down in private with me, and asked me about my service through the desert and Italy. A feeling of paralysis and stiffening had really become a problem, and he now told me that I should be down-graded to relieve me of any more front-line duty. I told him this was all very well, but there was no remedy to undo all that had been done to my whole system. At that, he decided to admit me to hospital, and I was sent to the 32nd British General Hospital in Belgium. I asked the major who took all my details what sort of treatment I would have, and he told me he'd have to give it some thought.

Within days, I was told I was to have ether treatment, and that was an unforgetable experience. The doctor told me to think back to Knightsbridge, when we lost our tank had to drag our bodies along the ground. Just at the appropriate time, he knocked me semi-conscious and asked me questions. Without hesitation, I screamed about coming out of the tank, passing the trench and being machine-gunned.

"How's the machine-gun now?" he asked. "Oh it's hellish!" I screamed. This only lasted about five minutes, but what a five minutes. It worked though, as I held nothing back, and remembered every detail and answered every question he asked. When it was over, I was sobbing my heart out, and buried myself in my pillow back in the ward for about half an hour.

I asked if another treatment was necessary, and was told that I couldn't expect all that had happened over three years to go away with one treament. Two days later I had ether treatment again with the same results, and I felt as if I was losing my senses. That didn't stop the same procedure again two days afterwards. The next week, the major changed to pentathol treatment, repeated three times in six days, but the effects were not nearly so severe. I got some peace after this, with only verbal interviews. There were many lads there with all sorts of complaints, and some were put to sleep for a week to ten days. I had been five or six weeks in hospital when news came that all who had been detained for more than thirty days were to have ten days home leave.

Soon I was back in Aberdeen, and after three days feeling pretty edgy, I went to Woolmanhill and was prescribed some pills which didn't do much for me at all. A couple of days later I went back and saw a psychiatrist who decided to admit me to a hospital in Larbert. Once there, I was allocated a specialist who took me over all my war history again. At least I felt at home in Larbert since I knew a few of my former customers there. I was referred to two more psychiatrists, but the talk in the hospital by now was that very few went out of there without their discharge. In my third week, I was given treatment with injections of insulin, which I got every morning for ten days. These had some effect, since the aim was to put on weight quickly. Within an hour of the injection we were ravenous, and heaped plates full of potatoes were served, with all the

extra sweetened juice we could drink to satisfy terrific thirst
and hunger. I hadn't realised I was under-weight, and I worried
that the insulin might have side-effects, but we had to leave it
to the experts.

Now we heard that a Board was to be convened to
regrade and discharge, and about twenty lads were notified for
interview. As each one came out, we asked what sort of questions were asked. "Oh it's easy," they replied, "do you like
trams, or do you like going on the buses?" This surprised me,
but I had all the answers ready, so I was shocked when the
chairman asked "Now, Sergeant McGregor, what do you think
caused this state?" "It all began at Knightsbridge," I replied,
"when our tank was hit and set on fire, and I had to drag my
body across the ground for four to five hours, being physically
and mentally shattered." "But you were a corporal then, and
now you're a sergeant, so you must have been doing your job
or you wouldn't have received promotion." I explained that
there had been little choice since we were so few in number
during the desert campaign. He asked me what I did in the
tank, and I told him I was a gunner in my first action at Fort
Capuso on June 4th. I told how we had to bale out after being
hit thirteen times by anti-tank shells. I was driver right up to
the fall of Tunis, and then tank commander for the invasion of
Italy and France. The secretary took notes of every word, as I
went on to tell of losing five tanks in the desert without even a
flesh wound. They asked me why I felt the need for treatment. I
explained the slow paralysis which I suffered. After a few more
questions the chairman said "I think we'll grant you your
discharge."

That was it, and I was suddenly on my way back to civvy
street. It was a very strange feeling, changing from uniform to
civilian clothes, as we were kitted out for going home. The
journey back was so different from others, which had been
merely a lull before going back into action. I was a married
man, and David my son was now a few months old. We had no
home, but Ina's folks had us live with them in Aberdeen, while

I tried to get so much out of my mind and settle down to a new existence. It was going to be very difficult, with so many looking for work in what was to me a strange new world altogether.

The egg business was now impossible though my brother had carried on as long as he could until eggs were restricted. I had to sign on at the Labour Exchange. I remember meeting Jim Burnett on our signing-on days when we could just about afford a cup of tea and a roll at the People's Cafe in the New Market.

Looking for something to do became quite demoralising, with so many chasing every single vacancy which arose in the papers. There was no easy solution, and my confidence wasn't helped when I met folk I knew who always asked if I wasn't working yet. After five months of signing on, I was interviewed by Willie Hutcheon, a wholesale grocer in Turriff, and Charles Alexander, the haulage contractor, with a view to my taking over the Ellon Stall at the New Market.

They had at that time two shops and an egg-grading station, but I was painfully aware that the grocery trade had drastically changed since my days in Kinmuck and Bainshole some ten years before. Rationing and scarcities meant little to me, but I got the job as manager although I had never seen a ration book or a Food Office form. My remuneration was £4 and ten shilllings per week and ten percent of the net profit, but money wasn't the main consideration since I had almost got to the stage of working for anyone for nothing, rather than be idle. The memory of those anxious days has given me a sympathy for those in the same plight today, and I don't take kindly to those who are so ready to condemn those who sign on "when they could be working". I reply "Just be careful. I was once in that situation, and there is nothing worse on this earth."

It may be of interest to record that, some two months after my discharge, I received word from the War Pension Office, awarding me 40 percent disability pension. This was done on the grounds that my latent neurosis, as it was termed, had been aggravated by war service, and I still wonder if that's why the Discharge Board was so hard on me. Another term for my illness was 'battle exhaustion', and when I contacted the British Legion to explain my situation they said the pension could be stopped any time. I asked their advice, and they told me that an attributable pension was for life, so they set the wheels in motion and an appeal was lodged.

A certificate from my family doctor was needed to ensure that there were no family origins for my illness. The appeal had to be heard in Edinburgh, and there I met the representative of the British Legion who was to put my case. My war history had hardly been presented by my representative before the chairman said that it was enough, and that the circumstances were quite straightforward. My appeal was granted.

The 40 percent remained in force for some years before being reduced to 30 percent, against which I again successfully appealed. Many years later, it was again reduced to 30 percent and I decided that enough was enough. The 30 percent award remains to this day, and I have no qualms whatsoever about receiving it, for all the years I have been tormented by nightmares of going into action all over again. Each day after one of these episodes, I am completely washed out, seeing that picture of the tanks ready to go into action and no doctor available for me to tell that I simply couldn't do it. The ether treatment I received at the 32nd General Hospital has not erased the dreams, but I know that we were really only guinea-pigs as psychoneurosis was only beginning to become accepted as an illness.

I feel so grieved when I remember the corporal who was sent out in charge of a patrol carrier in Italy. He came back saying he couldn't do it, but they sent him out again. Again he came back and they arrested him and put him in detention for 105 days in the rough hands of the military police. He was convicted of cowardice in face of the enemy and he was reduced to the ranks, but I know what he suffered. I too could have refused my superiors' orders, and no-one knew what it was to face the enemy with that crushing fear and paralysis.

I have heard tank crews talk about the hope of light wounds which would finish the war for them. I also knew of the wounds which were self-inflicted and were grave offences if detected. So I suppose we just soldiered on as one arm of the fighting troops, with so many hiding the fact that they were at breaking point. I do say, however, that many of us would have sacrificed an arm or leg to be relieved, especially when the alternative was so final a thing as death. At least in my time of need, such fears were understood and addressed, though far too late for many good men.

CHAPTER FOURTEEN

A New Career

I STARTED work on April 1st and I wonder if that was an omen, for I soon heard that the Ellon Stall, during the owner-ship of Willie Hutcheon and Charlie Alexander, had made no profit at all. There was a lot to be done, but it was amazing how things soon began to take shape, with a lot of attention due to the egg-grading station and the fresh foodstuffs.

There was a great shortage and restriction on many foodstuffs, and getting contacts for supplies was difficult. Some fruit was in allocation, but during the season there were good supplies of English fruits which were not by allocation. I became friendly with Willie Rezin who had a fruit wholesale business on the quay. He had been in business for a long time and had a big allocation of imported fruit. He was very good to me and gave me supplies of imported fruit to which I should not otherwise have been entitled. With a staff of five, therefore, we seemed to be justified. The original Ellon Stall, opposite the People's Cafe, was where most of the eggs came in from Ellon and was a popular place, well-known throughout Aberdeen for supplying good quality eggs. This stall was still only 22 feet by 11 feet and old Maggie had spent the greater part of her life there, a faithful servant who knew everybody. The other shop was about 1,000 square feet with a small selling area.

Although no profit showed on the the books for that first

financial year from my start on 1st April to December 1st, I received £25 for my effort in cleaning up the place. The shops seemed busy though, so I was hoping for better things in future. One day a chap in the shop asked for salad cream, and I told him we had none. "You've got it alright but you just won't sell it to me. It's a while in the front line you need." I couldn't believe it but I managed to ask him if three and a half years wasn't enough. It shook me to think how easily folk were prepared to hand out white feathers.

The days and months passed with weekly visits from Willie Hutcheon's inspector. He would arrive on Fridays at lunchtime and go through the weekly figures without much comment. When I took over, the overdraft was around £3,000, but I could see it gradually decrease on the bank statements. This was now 1948 and Mr Alexander came weekly to sign any cheques required, as well as being a helpful support for any ideas I wanted to try out. Willie Rezin continued to help me out with any good deals he found. One Thursday about lunchtime, he arrived with pears and peaches. I bought 30 small barrels of pears with 30 pounds in each, 20 baskets at 20 pounds each of English wine pears and 20 trays of 38 peaches. That was Thursday, and I had to purchase more before the end of the week. When you think of shifting over a half ton of pears in three days, there is some cause for satisfaction.

On another occasion he arrived on a Saturday morning with tomatoes. We were selling tomatoes at one shilling and seven pence per pound, and the cost from Willie was six pence per pound. I had 18 baskets in stock, so I bought 20 baskets and reduced my price to two pounds for one shilling and seven pence. By Saturday night I had sold 18 baskets which gave me the cost of my previous stock.

Now I found I was making three pence on every pound, and I bought 24 baskets on Monday and Tuesday, and 50 baskets on Wednesday so that I could still sell two pounds for one shilling and seven pence. By Saturday again I had to buy another 24 baskets to finish the day, making 144 baskets we sold in just one week, each basket weighing 12 pounds at three pence per pound profit. This caused great interest and customers were looking for more good bargain prices.

The following year had its unpleasantness. I knew Willie Hutcheon of Turriff had large supplies of fruit coming from England, and I got 400 pounds of plums delivered to me with skins all black. I phoned Mr Alexander and got his permission to dump them, writing to Turriff to this effect but receiving no reply. One Monday morning soon after, George Shand, the fruit man at Turriff, telephoned to sell me 50 cases of English apples, each case being 40 pounds in weight. He told me the price was ten pence per pound. I told him that Knowles at the end of the Market were selling Red English apples for ten pence per pound. After a pause it was Hutcheon who came on asking why I couldn't take the fifty cases. When I complained about quality, he said "You're not satisfied with the quality of my fruit? I'm not satisfied with the amount of business I'm getting from you and I'm coming down to see you. You're in for a disappointment."

In despair I contacted Mr Alexander and asked if it was the Ellon Stall or Hutcheon of Turriff I worked for. Alexander got in touch with Hutcheon and asked him if he wanted Mac to run the Stall and make a profit, or to get out of the partnership. Hutcheon chose to get out at that time, and Alexander announced that he was now my boss, which suited me as it would have had to be Hutcheon or me to go.

Within days, however, Charlie was back with the bad news that Hutcheon had backed out of the shares sale, saying the meeting was not properly constituted. I was told to give Hutcheon more business meantime but I reckoned Hutcheon would get rid of me before long. With only £613 between Ina and myself in the world, no house and no furniture, the future was not promising and I felt the way ahead was to try to get a business of my own.

CHAPTER FIFTEEN

My Own Wee Shop

I MADE enquiries about every shop which came on the market, picking up a good knowledge of values along the way. I went to see Webster's Grocer and Fruit Shop at 202 Holburn Street one Thursday night when I learned it had come on the market. Willie Webster was there with a Mr Ramsay from Storie Cruden Simpson, the estate agents, and we had a chat about things. The price was £2150, and since I only had £613 I needed help.

I signed for the shop on the Monday when Mr Ramsay came to see me at the Ellon Stall. He told me that as from that day I would get all the drawings, and have to pay all expenses for that week. As he left, Charlie Alexander happened to come in and remarked that I looked worried. When I told him I'd just signed for a shop he was speechless, and said that if he had been my sole boss I wouldn't be leaving now. I said bluntly that he hadn't done a lot to help me when I needed it and that I was leaving at the end of the week.

So the next chapter in my life began in June 1950, and I well remember standing in my shop that next Monday morning, with the prayer that I would be able to repay everything I owed. Willie Webster was a great chap, and had been a great businessman in his hey-day, although that was now passing. The shop had a big imported fruit allocation which was a great asset. Since much imported food was on points, the shop also had a big 'points bank'. With money borrowed to pay Willie, I hadn't a bean in the bank and only about a pound in my pocket. That Monday I received £125 which was the drawings less wages and expenses, so with less than £300 in stock there wasn't a lot to show for £2150 apart from a shop and ten year lease.

The front shop was roughly 139 square feet as was the back apartment, making it akin to two small rooms. That didn't worry me though, for all I could think about was making a go of it. Willie had let things go latterly so it wasn't too difficult to immediately raise the weekly income. Willie's brother Jim, who had a shop in Urquhart Road, popped in to see me and saw a big brass pot on the gas ring in the back shop. "This will be your best friend" he said, and it made me a lot of money. I took his advice and the brass pot was hardly ever cold as I boiled hams, beetroot and toffee, even though sugar was rationed.

I was so eager to make good that I was keen to pursue any suggestions from any quarter. A representative came one day and asked if I would buy some fondant. I was not completely ignorant but asked him what was the composition of the fondant and how could I make use of it. He gave me the analysis; the fondant consisted of sugar, glucose and water. I bought a 56 pound box and put some into the big brass pan. It was so much easier to melt than sugar. When it was liquid and boiling I added some Nestle's milk. With no experience to help me, I boiled it for a while, then when it was off the boil I stirred it for some time. There was no sign of the mixture sugaring so after some time I gave up and proceeded to scrape it into the bucket.

As I scraped, the mixture was beginning to turn to sugar or toffee. It was too late to salvage any of it, but I hoped to learn by my mistake and I tried another boiling of fondant and Nestle's milk. Leaving the pan off the gas after what I thought looked like the right colour and consistency, I stirred it well and this time it was a success. It tasted so good I knew I could find a market for it. The customers loved it and I would make a boiling at 6 o'clock in the morning and another after I closed at 6 o'clock at night. It had to be done when the back shop was clear to get all the trays laid out to take 60 pounds of toffee. I had a pal, Athol Lumsden, no longer with us, and he was keen to help and said that as I sold his biscuits, he would try to sell my toffee. This was a most successful venture and although it had me working from early morning until late at night, I did not mind for I had no other interests. My total expense was my tram fares and while I had obligations I had to be careful with money.

I had no big plans for building the business at this time, for all I wanted to do was pay everyone back. There were no ideas of cars and houses, or long holidays. I did what I knew best - buying good quality stock and selling at reasonable prices. Willie Webster had not packed his own dried cereals such as split peas, barley, lentils and so on, or dried fruits like raisins, currants, figs and dates. Robert Duthie, the wholesale grocer, was the expert in these matters, and it wasn't long before my customers were enjoying such quality goods, thanks to the advice and help of this honest, straightforward and totally reliable man. I had another good friend in my jar of whiting and a brush. While it would be frowned upon today perhaps, I had great fun each morning painting my windows with adverts about the goods and prices I was offering. Trade grew quickly, and I remember having takings of £200 in a week and thinking I could buy half of Aberdeen. I suppose the equivalent today would be about £10,000 so it wasn't bad going for a wee shop of 139 square feet.

I had two girls working with me, and within three weeks one of the girls I had employed on the Ellon Stall came to join us. We were kept busy and trade increased week by week. The smallness of the shop never bothered or restricted me, for I never accepted any limitations. I used the front of the window outside for displays, and the doorway was always filled with fruit and vegetables. I think I was the first in Aberdeen to enter

the 'keen prices' market, and I remember buying 60 dozen
Sunshine bleach, having it delivered as required, and I could
now sell it at the price I had to pay buying by the dozen. This
whetted my appetite for this type of trading, especially as
goods which had been scarce were gradually coming back.

Mr Donald, who was representative for Crosse and
Blackwell Chef products, produced a bottle of Chef brown
sauce which had been in short supply. The price was ten pence
a bottle, and the first thing I asked was what he would do if I
sold it at a shilling a bottle. He simply said he would be back
for another order. I asked because it was possible that other
shopkeepers would refuse his trade if he dealt with me on such
terms. It was cut-throat stuff.

I was using every inch of floor space with displays five
foot high, and sometimes I paid the penalty. I had bought 24
dozen jars of marmalade to sell at a shilling a jar, and I made a
circular floor display to a height of about five feet. It sold like
hotcakes, but a tin falling from a shelf on to the display
wrecked eleven jars. All I did was rebuild the display and
recoup the loss by selling even more jars.

I must recall my first Christmas when I took the opportunity to shed stock I had taken over when I bought the shop. I
bought 1,000 sheets of Christmas wrapping and parcelled up
those goods which were unrationed and points-free. I filled five
big apple barrels with one-shilling, two-shilling and half-crown
parcels, and by the end of the New Year I had got rid of all
surplus stock. The apples had come from Willie Rezin again,
and I had put the barrels at the door with a big ticket. We sold
eight barrels, each of some ten stone of first quality apples.

Every inch of the shop was used for display, and it was
so good to see piles of groceries all with big sales tickets. I just
wanted the shop to look alive, and the bonus was that those
who came to buy loved my 'wee shoppie'.

It was all hard graft, but I had not been fooled by the
belief that we had a 'land fit for heroes to live in'. As far as I
could see, you had to be a hero just to exist, and I knew that

nothing simply fell into your lap if you sat back and waited. The *Evening Express* started a 'Housewife's Choice' page, and since the advertising was quite reasonable, I took a weekly space. I included in my advert my motto "Wise Spending is Good Housekeeping". This became a regular talking point. The response was very encouraging, and I eventually had to fit slip-on hinges to the door, since customers were often getting trapped behind it in the crush. On Thursdays, Fridays and Saturdays, I could now simply lift the door off the hinges and put it into the back shop.

One Saturday morning a customer counted 22 people packed into the wee shop, but it was all taken in good part, and we had a lot of fun over it. One Saturday, when the customers couldn't get in to the shop, and once in could hardly get out again, and the till was going on fine style, one of the girls said "If you advertise next week we won't be here". "But I've suffered too," I replied "so we'll give it a break."

All the world was at peace. After some years, Mr Young came from Storie Cruden Simpson to ask if I wanted to buy my shop. The price was £900, and my first reaction was that it was impossible, so little did I think I was making. I just worked away from 7.00 am till 9 or 10 o'clock at night. It was eight years before I took a holiday - Monday, Tuesday and Wednesday in a pre-fab in Finzean. I was back in the shop on Thursday morning. I reckon as I look back, that it wouldn't suit many people these days, but obligations to many people gave me little option. I purchased my shop and looked at the piece of ground next to it belonging to my neighbouring shopkeeper, Willie Allan the butcher. I had now been in business for nine years, and I made a financial arrangement with Willie Allan for this 14 foot by 12 foot area. It meant I could make a proper store, and then enlarge the shop itself by knocking down the wall between the front and back apartments. That I immediately arranged.

We tried to cover the stock as best we could, before the builder arrived about 10 pm on the Saturday night. Standing on the opposite pavement, it was hours before I could see into the shop again for dust. The steel beam was in place before 3 am that Sunday morning, making my shop twice the size at some 312 sqare feet. I had arranged with the joiner to fix shelves in what had been the back shop, in preparation for the wall coming down. They had finished by midnight on Friday, so all it needed was decoration to make it part of the new shop. I set about it with a gallon of white emulsion, finishing by 4.30 am on Saturday morning.

The girls worked hard and we had the holiday weekend to stock the shelves over Sunday and Monday. Our new counter was 18 feet long, and the results were immediate with our customers having 'room to change their minds'. In time, there were ten assistants behind the counter on a Saturday morning, yet many a time the customers couldn't all get into the shop at once.

CHAPTER SIXTEEN

The New Way to Shop

TRADING CONDITIONS were changing constantly with the passing years, and for some time a salesman for self-service fittings had been pestering me. I reckoned it was madness since there wasn't a self-service shop in Aberdeen, but it niggled at me. I felt the pressure of staffing when one assistant, taking too many days off, put considerable strain on the others. I saw no end to this problem with counter service so I took the plunge. What really convinced me happened one morning in the shop about 7.30 am. A customer bought a tin of peas, a packet of custard and a box of matches, and when I reckoned the profit to be a few pennies I knew it was time to let my customers do the walking and choosing. There were no guarantees, but the few trusted friends I spoke to warned me I must 'sell' the idea and I felt I could do just that.

The weekend of the changeover was again a holiday weekend and, now in 1962, I had been in business for about twelve years. When the shop closed on the Saturday night at 6.00 pm I had a Clark and Rose lorry booked to be at the door. All groceries had to be packed and loaded along with all the fittings. By 10.30 pm that night all the walls were bare, and the shop and windows had to be cleaned for Tuesday opening. Next came the painting, and new linoleum to be laid by Sainsbury next door. The job was finished by 5.30 am on

Sunday morning, and by 8.30 am the van with the new shop fittings was at the door. The new self-service shelves and cash points were in place by 10.30 am, giving us the rest of Sunday and Monday to lay out stock prior to opening on Tuesday morning.

That fateful morning I was standing at the door of the shop, having told the girls I wasn't answering the phone to anyone. The first reactions were not so good, with customers feeling that they didn't want to use a basket. I told them they didn't need to, but I wanted them to look around and tell me what they thought of the new shop. That did it, and our sales were almost doubling, but I didn't leave that shop door for three weeks.

The days passed, the response was still good, and fellow grocers used to stand on the pavement outside, wondering - as I knew they would - whether this was going to be a glorious success or a notable failure. We never looked back, and it was a good feeling to know that I had successfully launched one of the first self-service shops in Aberdeen. There was no reduction of staff, rather better deployment, with the preparation of pre-packaged goods being a major task. I well recall the first forenoon when I noticed a pile of baskets at the cash-out, and realised that they were using them at last.

At this time, there was a buying group of independent grocers in Aberdeen and outlying districts. I had meantime joined up with Bill Luke in Skene Square, and Alick Christie in Park Street, both of whom had the same trading attitudes as me. We were making our own small impact, and I recall our purchase of oatcakes with a five-penny coupon attached to each packet. We removed the coupons and sold the oatcakes for a penny a packet, which drew rumours that we had stolen the oatcakes. We laughed at that and sold hundreds of cartons, but I still had this burning desire to expand.

I was looking for any building I could convert into a shop when as luck would have it Charlie Alexander advertised for a manager for the Ellon Stall. He was sole owner now since

Hutcheon had eventually sold his shares for a half crown each. When you think that he sent back Alexander's offer of ten shillings per share all that time ago, you have to believe that some folk will never learn.

I phoned Charlie and suggested that as he was better at lorries than dealing with sugar and tea, he should sell the Ellon Stall to me. He refused to leave a sinking ship, as he called it, but he offered me the chance to buy shares. He didn't have long to wait for my reply, and he gave me the keys to the two shops at the Market four days later. I enquired about the financial position and was told that the overdraft was now between £17,000 and £18,000, although it had been down to £500 when I left to go to Holburn Street. I shudder to think what that overdraft would be in today's figures but all I looked at was the challenge this presented.

I was in the Market by 8.30 am on Tuesday morning to open the two shops, and there as always, was faithful Maggie staffing one shop while a girl was looking after the other. I looked round and was far from impressed. I told Charlie the bigger shop would need refitting - for starters. He asked me who would do it, and I recommended Salemaster shop-fittings, phoning Robin Rennie, their representative, right away. He came up from Tillycoutry the next day, and we signed for the new fittings.

The shop was to be refitted the next weekend, and come Saturday night I closed my shop in Holborn Street and went straight to the New Market. All stock had to be removed from the shop, but there was plenty of floor space in the Market for the groceries and fittings. The manager and I were pushing fittings to one end of the Market at 1.30 am in the morning, and the fitters were there ready to make the installations. I left the New Market at 2.30 am on Sunday morning leaving the fitters to get on with their work, telling them I'd see them at 7.30 am that morning. By 8.30 am the manager, staff and myself were ready to fill the new shelves. It was quite a marathon, with a new refrigerator to be installed as well.

We had a busy day, but by 1.30 am on the Monday morning, the shelves were full, the fridge installed and the prices on display. It looked good. Mind you, Ian Law, our new manager from Peterhead, had no experience of self-service shops, so I stayed Monday, Tuesday and Wednesday to break him in.

It was quite an experience to see the customers' faces when they saw the total change in the shop since Saturday, and even if I say so myself, it really looked good. Now that the big shop was under way, I turned my attention to the stall opposite the People's Cafe. Charlie Alexander asked me what I intended to do about it, and I replied "I'm closing it on Saturday."

Well, Maggie was due to retire, and my idea was to have it as a provisions shop selling only cheeses, cooked meats, bacon and pies. Two large refrigerators were installed which completely filled the back of the stall, while the rest of the shop was fitted with white formica shelves to take the cheeses and so on. Charlie had said nothing about my plans, and when he had expressed doubt about my closing the shop I had simply said that I had the keys and it would close on Saturday night.

It was three weeks before it was refitted and ready to open, and my only instruction to the manager was to sell only provisions such as the meats and cheeses. Ian was a great worker and both shops were a huge success. Although it took time, before long there was a queue every Saturday morning for bacon, pies and the like.

I had inceased the overdraft to £24,000 which was a terrifying figure in 1962, and would be even more so today. Within eight years, however, we had a credit of £5,000 in spite of all the work which was required and the necessary increase in staffing. Every member of staff worked hard and deserved the highest praise. It was all very satisfying, and although it was a very long time indeed before I was in a position to receive my director's fees, the sight of these shops doing roaring trade was far more important and fulfilling than money.

Meanwhile my shop at 202 Holburn Street was ticking

over nicely, and after digesting the purchase of the shop for £900, I still had the courage to get a place to live. A building licence was needed, and I purchased a feu in Cults Gardens where I built a house. I got some wisecracks about choosing Cults, but my reply was that it was as easy to build a house in Cults as in the Hardgate, but when it was finished it would be worth at least a half more. It made sense to me as a good investment and safeguard for the future, and so the four-roomed detached house was built in 1963 at a cost of £1878, of which I paid £409 as a deposit. It costs a little more today, but that doesn't put money in the pocket and it's still my home. Life, as they say, is full of horizons, and they just keep coming.

CHAPTER SEVENTEEN

McGregor's Self-Service

MEANWHILE THINGS were changing in Holburn Street. The Holburn Bar built new premises next to the old one, and as I walked past I measured roughly the side down Strachan Lane. It was 84 yards, and I thought what a super shop it would make, but the size alone made it seem foolish to think about purchasing it. The years passed, and it was still empty, and there were rumours that a supermarket was to purchase it, which sent shivers down my spine. One Monday morning, I was washing my shop window when Noel Sainsbury, of the furniture shop next door, came over. I asked him why he hadn't thought about buying the old bar. "Same reason as you, Mac, money, which I don't have."

Suddenly something clicked amongst the sawdust of my brain, and I realised the bar might be unsold because everyone assumed the cost would be prohibitive. I phoned my good friend and lawyer Bill Crosby, who was amazed at what I was thinking. Nevertheless he got the keys and we went to see the premises. Bill's first comment was that they *were* big enough. Noel Sainsbury had reckoned the asking price would be between £12,000 and £18,000, which were figures well out of my reach. Still I thought to test the water and asked Bill to make an offer of £6,000. He laughed, but within three weeks he was signing for the purchase of the old Bar on my behalf.

I seriously believe that this was the property bargain of
the year. No sooner had it been signed over to me than I received an offer of £12,000. Bill believed that if I made a go of
things here I could easily double that figure. The Saturday after
the price was settled, I was in the Royal Bank southern branch
when I met the manager, Mr Rae. The conversation developed
along these lines: "Any word of that Holburn Bar property
yet?" "Yes. It's been sold." "And who on earth has bought it?"
"I have for £6,000." "Just how are you going to finance it?"
"I'm hoping that you'll help." Some time before, Mr Rae had
indicated in somewhat fanciful terms that he would 'walk on
his head' to have my account and finance me if I needed it, so
this was his chance to make good his words.

I really didn't need such an awful lot, for I had my
original Holburn Street shop to sell, as well as ground and an
old building with two small shops right across the road. I had
bought this building for £550 when it was condemned for
occupation, and used it as a store. It was a big feu, and I had
reckoned it might be useful someday. The town put a compul-

sory purchase order on this ground as they wanted it for car parking for the new College of Commerce being constructed. I had an offer of £2,000 and Bill Crosby said that he would seek an increase in this offer. I wasn't too worried, for I reckoned my Holburn shop would fetch about £2,500, and with the purchase order from the town of £2,000 it wouldn't leave such a big balance anyway. I was buying a big and valuable building, and I knew that Aitken the baker was after a shop in Holburn Street.

Sure enough, through my friend Stan Imray of Mollisons, I sold the shop to Aitken for the said £2,500 - drawing the comment from Bill Crosby that "If you fell in a sewer, you'd come up with a goldfish."

Still, there were plenty of intial worries, since the payment for the new shop had to be made by June. There was also much to be done to the shop itself, since the frontage of about 40 feet had to be taken out to put in large windows and two doors. Since I had given Aitken the baker November for entry, I couldn't get my money until occupation.

Meantime the work had to go on in the new shop, and if the frontage was a big project, the inside was even more terrifying. I had to get rid of the smoky smell, and prepare the floor for laying, removing many thousands of nails over many hours. I went home so many nights with an aching back, but the good antidote to this pain was my main contractor, Alick Farquhar, who had a gift for dispelling difficulties. We needed all our time before November, rewiring and installing the new lighting before putting in all the fittings. Unhappily, fittings from the old shop were not nearly enough to equip this larger area - 1500 sqare feet in the front and again in the back - so I had to invest in extra fittings.

When the time for opening drew near, I had no doubts about who should 'do the honours' and asked an eighty year old customer, Mrs.Waterton from Howburn Place. I didn't think to invite some 'personality' for it had to be someone who represented what I wanted the shop to be - the family's own store. Before the great event there was a lot to be done, especially washing and cleaning, to get rid of the smell of smoke. The floor laying was a big operation, but Noel Sainsbury was equal to the task, while Blake was sub-contracted to do the shop front amongst other things.

When the big windows were fitted, I began to think of it at last as a shop, but we now had only one week to get fittings in and stock the shelves. We used the same procedure as we had at number 202 when we changed from counter to self-service, and we had Clark and Rose's furniture van at the door by 6.00 am on the Saturday evening. All stock was transferred to the van which was garaged for the night. We scrubbed and cleaned until 3.30 am on Sunday morning, noticing the curious on-lookers grow fewer and fewer as the wee small hours came. We were growing more tired by the minute. The fittings from number 202 were to be brought over, not that they would make much impact in this shop, coming from 612 square feet to 1500 square feet. The fittings were to be delivered on the Sunday morning at 7.30 am, and I was there at that time, joined by the staff at 8.30 am. There was no sign of the fittings at 9.00 am nor at 10.00 am nor at 11.00 am. We were short of time with the shop due to open on Thursday, and we spent the waiting time getting as much stock into the front shop as possible, ready for the big fill. The lorry arrived at 12.30 pm by which time I was really in some panic.

We'd been told that very few people walked on our side of the street, and I reckon more than a few people were hoping that our shop would be a white elephant. Still, I was confident we could make it work. I took out a full-page advertisement in the *Evening Express* as there is always some interest in a new shop, and there were the usual incentives of some free boxes of fruit and bunches of flowers. I pay tribute once more to my staff who worked so hard and long to enable me to see this dream become a reality. The Lord alone knows where we got the strength to work on, and many a night I felt faint as I left the shop after midnight. Indeed a friend of mine with considerable medical knowledge said that if I'd kept this up for much longer, I wouldn't have been around for the opening.

By the Wednesday night, however, we had done enough, and Mrs Waterton was to be ready to do the official opening at 9.00 on the Thursday morning. I had booked a Wedding Taxi '777' from City Taxis to collect Mrs Waterton and travel up Great Western Road, past the lights on Anderson Drive, down Broomhill Road, Anderson Drive again to Bridge of Dee, then slowly along Holburn Street to the new shop. I had put a special poster on the taxi which read: "This Taxi is going to the Opening of McGregor's New Shop at 219 Holburn Street." With this extra piece of advertising, some twenty or so people were waiting at the shop to see Mrs Waterton cut the ribbon.

I had urged my lassies to try and make sure that for every

Mrs Waterton opening the shop at 219 Holburn Street

five customers who found their way to the shop, two or three would want to come back. We were very, very busy that first day, and had a most satisfactory Thursday, Friday and Saturday, but I was waiting for a new week before I put the flags out. The grocery trade is no bonanza, but through the process of building the business, I still had confidence that all would be well. It was certainly a change to operate in premises of 1500 sqare feet, a back shop of the same proportions, coming from 612 square feet at number 202. As I looked, on one of those first days, from front shop to back shop, I wondered "Duncan, do you think you're the part for this?" I had an uncle who had many couthy sayings, and one such was "Better a small fire to warm you, than a big one to burn." I often thought had I not got a directorship in the Ellon Stall, I might well have overstretched myself and been unable to cope. Still, all that is history now.

Days and weeks passed, and we enjoyed the luxury of such a big shop in which to work and where we could test so many selling techniques. I no longer left my shop to see how the other half of the world was behaving, and the four walls at number 219 became my life. I believed that people wanted

The new shop

better space to shop in, and I felt I had made the right move at
the right time. I once read a book called 'Turning Points in
Successful Careers' and reckoned that this had been my turning
point. I spent most of my time in the front shop, speaking to as
many customers as possible, and I had increased both range
and quantity of stock, so that folk could more easily find what
they wanted. I was always carrying boxes of goods to customers' cars, just as a good public relations exercise, and it was
much appreciated.

The back shop had built-in refrigerated units which
looked quite impressive, and I cooked hams which I swear
tasted different from factory produce or tinned meats. We
purchased the best in bacon, and I was always particular about
the quality of my purchases. I remember an offer of bacon from
a certain supplier which was a silly low price compared with
what I was used to paying elsewhere. I had often wondered
how the big shops were able to sell bacon at such low prices,
so I asked him to send me a roll of Ayrshire bacon. When it
arrived, I cut 20 to 30 slices, and fried them in the staffroom,
before offering a taste to the lassies and some of the customers.
I quite often did this as my own kind of market research.
Nobody liked it any more than I did, and one bacon customer
actually said that it certainly wasn't our bacon. I asked myself
what I should do with this roll, and decided to hang it in the
fridge before finally giving it away. At least I did not lose any
of my customers by selling them this poor stock.

I've not often had the good fortune to get something for
nothing, or rather to get something with no effort on my part,
but on one occasion a customer won the 'Chimp Chat' Brooke
Bond Tea competition for Scotland and received £500. As the
grocer who sold her the tea I got the grocer's prize of £50 and
had to go to Glasgow along with the customer to receive my
cheque. John Gray, the Brooke Bond salesman who sold the
tea, was invited to the presentation and we were treated lav-
ishly. The highlight of the event was to see the monkeys at
close range and also to see how kindly they were treated.

Duncan with the Brooke Bond chimps

With the big back shop came a cold room which had been in use for the bar. It was about as big as my wee shop at number 202, so I had it reduced to 12 feet square, and had the benefit of cooling units already in place to keep our provisions in first-class condition. We needed no inspectors to tell us how to preserve our goods, and we had plenty of room to pack our dried cereals and fruits. I bought the biggest prunes available from Alick Duthie, and what a joy it was to deal with someone who knew his trade so well, and took a pride in what he stocked. Of course, Alick's father had been in the trade all his life, and had established a wholesale grocery and warehouse. And now Alan Duthie, Alick's son is keeping the family flag flying.

Having goods delivered now was so easy, and not the hassle I'd been used to: getting goods at the front and having to carry them through the shop to the back. We now had a side entrance for goods, off Strachan's Lane, which ran up the side of the shop from the Hardgate to Holburn Street, and could accommodate any size of lorry. We made some large purchases, such as half a ton of butter and 500 boxes of cake after the New Year, but the major buy was a lorry load of goods from a failed company. The total cost was less than half the real value, and the quality was excellent.

It was so good to work with a fine bunch of girls, all six of them, who were always so agreeable and helpful. Some people said we were just like a big family, and I would dare to say we were happier than most families. There was never nastiness or trouble, although I'm sure there were times when they could have seen me in 'the bad place', or I them. Such feelings were never put into words, for it was my philosophy that a spoken word could never be taken back, no more than you could rescind a hurtful action. Life is all too short to quarrel, and I would always say to any new assistant I was taking on "This place can be heaven or hell. Please try to make it heaven." This created a pleasant atmosphere which my customers still remember today after 15 years in number 202 and 20 years in number 219.

CHAPTER EIGHTEEN

Customer Self-Service

NOWADAYS SHOPLIFTING is taken very seriously, and much need, but when I started the little shop in the early fifties, shoplifting was hardly heard of, or at least it was not taken as a grave danger to trading. My first experience happened in the small shop one Friday morning. We were fairly busy and I saw this lady taking three packets of Simmers butter biscuits and putting them in her message bag. I could hardly believe my eyes when she then walked out of the shop. I took several minutes to think and by the time I decided I must do something about it, the lady was about 100 yards down the street. However I forced myself to go after her and when I caught up I tried to see if there was anything in her bag. Knowing I couldn't let it go without checking, I approached her and said "You didn't pay for the butter biscuits you put in your shopping bag." "Oh," she said "did I not pay for them?" I replied "I'll just take payment now," and she paid the sum I requested.

I was inexperienced then, but I would have said this lady was the last person I expected to steal; a respectably dressed, well-spoken person who to my mind did not need to steal. Experience showed that it was often the most unlikely people who had this weakness for shoplifting.

When we moved across the street to the big shop with a selling area of 1500 square feet, I was advised to cover most of the shop with cameras. Three cameras were installed but experience taught me that they were only effective when someone was watching them constantly, which could be quite expensive. However they were very good when someone was acting suspiciously and we would put the camera on them to watch what they did.

Experience also taught me to recognise people who were likely to steal, people who, previously, I would never have suspected. All the staff were aware that a customer could be stealing, and with around nine of us continually on the move in the shop, it was amazing how much we saw. The obvious culprits were those with a message bag along with their basket, or people with a loose coat and 'poacher' pockets. The first lady we caught in the big shop had shopped with us nearly every morning. One of the girls saw something which didn't look quite right so we put the camera on her. Being my first culprit in the new shop, it required all my courage to see her through the cash desk, then call her back (that was the procedure which had to be adopted). When I took her through to the office there were splashes of tears and a funny mixture of excuses. Her booty was £3 odds and I remember her words "I'm not short of money." She had about £10 in her purse. I tried to explain to her that the reason she had money in her purse might be that she didn't pay for the goods she carried home. That was the end of her custom - by my request.

The majority of shoplifters, when asked through to the office, admitted their wrongdoing. It was difficult to know just how far to pursue the matter without bringing in the police but I used to try to handle each incident myself first, and try to come to some understanding with the culprit. When I had ample proof the person had been stealing persistently, I asked him or her to come to my office. "Have you anything in your bag or on your person for which you did not intend paying, say around £2 worth of goods?" I would then say "This is not the first time you have tried to leave the shop with goods which you haven't paid for." Then my next line, "Are you prepared to pay an estimate of the total goods you have taken?" I might suggest three weeks to pay £2 a week or £6 right away. It was amazing how many paid a few pounds, rather than face the police. I found that police detectives were often *not* the best way to deal with minor offences.

One man we spotted had pockets full of biscuits, sultanas, soft biscuits, packets of nuts and tins of fruit. We had to let him pass the till and leave the shop. I went out after him and asked him to come back in. As soon as he entered the door he threw out everything he had in his pockets. It was almost funny seeing tins of fruit, packets of biscuits, bags, nuts and other things strewn all over the shop floor. What could I do in this situation? He had no goods on his person and I hadn't lost anything. After this incident, when I was taking someone through to the office, I always walked behind them.

On another occasion, a school boy about 15 years old, had some groceries in his pocket which he hadn't paid for. He had a bicycle outside the shop and when I followed him outside and said I would like to speak to him, back in the shop, he grabbed his bicycle and tried to get away. Whilst I was trying to hold his cycle back, he started kicking savagely and I wasn't able to hold him. One night after school, this same boy had about ten bars of chocolate in his pocket. When he left the shop without paying I said I would like to speak to him. He made to bolt and I caught hold of his pocket, the one which contained the chocolate. His blazer ripped right up to his shoulder. I would like to know what he told his parents but I guess it wasn't the truth. He got away but it was rather expensive chocolate.

One Friday afternoon some of the girls happened to be looking at a camera and saw a man filling his pocket with Rennies tablets. On such occasions I stayed very near the till and if possible I tried to cash out the offender myself. I had two tills and on this occasion there were about ten customers in the queue. The culprit gave me his basket and I checked the goods in it and gave him his change. I wasn't following the book when I said to him "Are you not going to pay for the packets of Rennies you have in your pocket?" He produced twenty-one packets. To teach him a lesson I said quite loudly "It's a good thing that all the customers around here don't do this or we won't be in business very long." I made him pay for the twenty-one packets, or rather I said to him "You'll be paying for the Rennies."

Another incident involved a customer who came regularly to the shop several times a week. The girls had their suspicions that she was putting things into her pocket. After a week or so, having taken note of what she had *not* paid for, I allowed her to go out of the shop one day and followed her. I said "Can I speak to you?" "Oh, what's the matter?" she replied. I said "My girls tell me you are putting articles in your pocket and not paying for them at the cash desk." "Oh," she said "I wouldn't do that to you." I replied "What about that tin of spam you have in your left hand coat pocket?" She produced the tin of spam. I asked her to come to the office and have a chat. I produced the list of all we had seen her put in her pocket during the week saying "This is a list of the goods you have taken and not paid for over the past week. Would you like to pay for them now?" She was delighted to part with the amount saying "I'm not short of money." This was a comment I received several times from different people. Finally, she said "I *will* come back to the shop." I said "Certainly come, for we all like to see you." Needless to say she did not come back. With older people I never used to call the police, but tried to find some method of getting them to own up to what they had stolen and agree to a figure. I found this very successful and the offenders usually avoided the shop afterwards.

Another very interesting case was that of a lady who took a few pounds worth of chocolate and sweets without paying for them. When I spoke to her in the office, she said "This is the first time I've done this." She seemed an intelligent person so I tried another approach, saying "If you were standing in my place now, and I told you this story, would you believe me?"

She paid me all the money she had and she was £1 short of the price of the sweets she had taken. She promised to pay me as soon as she could. This was Friday night and on Monday I had a £1 note and a lovely letter (with her letterhead removed) from her saying "Thankyou so much for Friday night - you taught me something I'll never forget." I never wanted to demolish anyone if it could be avoided.

Each experience was different. One Saturday night about 5 o'clock, a man asked if we had any cooked chickens. I told him they were in the fridge. He disappeared for some time and came back to the cash desk. I said to him "Didn't you find the chickens?" His reply was "I'll not bother tonight." He had a bulge in his coat and I suspected it was a chicken. What was I to do? He seemed to me to be a nasty individual, and I had not the slightest doubt that if I accused him he would hit me and perhaps put me through the window. So rather than risk landing in the casualty department I let him go with my chicken. Being badly hurt wasn't worth the price of the chicken.

I had another nasty experience. I employed Group 4 at different times, just to give me some assurance that stealing was not getting out of hand. The Group 4 girl caught a man stealing gammon steaks and some bacon. She tackled him outside the shop but he refused to come back in and threw the bacon and the gammon steaks at her in the street. About a year later, on a Saturday night between 5 and 6 o'clock, this same man was standing in front of the shop. He said "I want to speak to you. You and that b.. f.. c.. of a girl accused me of stealing gammon steaks some time ago. Well," he said, and pointed to his chin, "the dark nights are coming and I'll be looking after you." He had a car and I took down the registration number and gave it to the police. Fortunately, he was known to one of the policemen who went out, found him and told him that if he was seen within half a mile of Holburn Street he would be charged. This incident was always in my mind and on the dark nights I never came out of the shop alone.

One of the most blatant examples of willful stealing I

met was when a mother and daughter came shopping together. They came from Bloomfield and were well known. We all suspected they were stealing and one Saturday we were determined to catch them. There was a bell on each till and we had made up codes so that different numbers of rings of a bell meant different things. Four rings was the sign that someone was up to something. This day when the four rings came, we had all planned different observation positions. It was not long before mother's and daughter's baskets were almost full. I said to the girls "That's enough now, I'll take over." I reckoned I was in command of the situation. Some time later as I was waiting for them to come to the cash desk, the mother arrived with only a bag of sugar and a toilet roll in her basket. I wasn't so clever; there was no sign of the daughter with her basket of groceries.

I left the shop behind the mother to see where she would go. She went toward Great Southern Road with me fairly close behind her, and stopping at the side of the street, suddenly she began to cross Fonthill Road. Then I saw the daughter across the road going towards the Hardgate. I had to negotiate the traffic and it took me a while before I could get across Fonthill Road, then Great Southern Road. By this time the daughter had seen me and was running with her bag of my groceries. I was doing the four minute mile, but with the start she had I was going to have difficulty catching her.

A car was coming up the Hardgate so I stopped the driver and asked if he could help me to catch this girl with the bag of groceries she hadn't paid for. He obliged and we just caught up with her before she got into her house in Bloomfield. She no longer had the spoils, but the driver of the car said he had seen a bag of groceries lying on the road in the Hardgate. I told the girl she would need to come back to the shop. We walked back to where the messages had been dropped and eventually the mother joined us, so now there was mother, daughter, the car and myself standing in the street in the Hardgate. The two culprits did not want to come back to the shop with me until I said "Well, we'll just make a show of this in the middle of the street, and I'll tell everyone what has been going on." They eventually agreed and we made our way back to the shop. I got them, most reluctantly, into my office, locked us all in and phoned the police. They had arranged to see friends in Peterhead and I would not wish to print the names they called me. The police eventually arrived, took a statement, then took mother and daughter to the Police Station. They had had about £14 of my groceries in their bag and subsequently they were convicted and fined. I cannot say it was a happy ending but at least it was one evil we got rid of.

I could not recall all the instances of shoplifting I experienced but the cases I have described give an indication of how difficult and even dangerous, shop life can be.

CHAPTER NINETEEN

Vacation on the QE2

SHOP LIFE was not always toil and worry; every year I had two weeks away from business. I am an impetuous person and I had a great longing to sail on the QE2. One year, having the time and such strong desire, I booked myself a seven-day voyage to America, a 36-hour stay in New York and the return voyage. It was a fascinating time, seeing how the rich live. A highlight of the voyage was the captain's party; that was a show I'll never forget. So many ladies dripping with furs, gold and diamonds. As I was alone I just concentrated on the trip being a lesson on how others live.

I believe many people think of a voyage on the QE2 as the opportunity to eat all the finest food that can be had. It is true that the finest food is available - caviar in abundance - in fact the QE2's consumption of caviar is a big percentage of the entire world supply. After a few days I had had so much to eat that instead of looking forward to the next meal, I had to search the menu for something small and light. Lobster was on the menu sometimes and I was anxious to try it. My worry was that I didn't know how to begin to eat it. One lady at the table ordered lobster and I watched her with great interest. She ate the red parts along with two blobs of sauce on her plate. After this demonstration I was ready to tackle the animal, however it was coming to the end of the trip before it appeared again on the menu and by this time I wasn't able to eat such a rich

Boarding the QE2 at Southampton

meal. I suppose it was a lost opportunity. I remembered the two shillings of boiling beef which fed us for four days at Bainshole; this was the opposite but which would do the body more good?

It can be said with truth that there was almost nothing that one desired that could not be supplied by the QE2. Breakfast would be anything from roast beef to a boiled egg. Morning coffee was available all over the ship. Lunch, at about one o'clock was as substantial as a dinner. Afternoon tea was served all over the ship and included the most beautiful cakes, each one must have had thousands of calories. Dinner followed in the evening and with such a menu. There were two waiters for every seven guests so you can imagine how well we were catered for. There was a swimming pool on the ship, sun beds all over the deck and every kind of entertainment you can think of available. There were bars, several dance floors with live dance bands, and every night the music continued well into the next morning.

At the captain's party on the homeward voyage, I got

Ready for dinner

into conversation with two others who, like myself, were travelling alone. We arranged to meet before dinner for a drink. We were all at different tables for dinner but that didn't need to stop us meeting for a drink during the evening. Mary was on her way to Belgium to a conference for linguists and Roderick had business to do in London regarding property. What impressed me a great deal was that nearly all the Americans seemed to be so well-off; I never got round to discussing their earnings compared with the British standard, but my guess was that they were much higher. Nearly all the passengers on board were American.

Reflecting on the lavish living I was enjoying made me think of the not-so-good times, such as arriving in Larbert without enough money to pay our digs if we didn't sell any eggs, or of one day after I had joined the First Royal Tank Regiment in Egypt when I didn't have a piaster to buy myself a cup of tea at break time. On that occasion, Harold Hadden from Dunfermline had come to my aid saying "Are you skint Mac? Come on, I have some piasters." Again, when I signed the cheque for Willie Webster for 202 Holburn Street, I think I may have had £2 in my pocket. I think it's good to have experienced the depths, then the good times mean so much more. I am so grateful and thankful for so many blessings of good health and good fortune.

CHAPTER TWENTY

Retiral from Holburn Street

IN 1977 I retired because of a function of the City of Aberdeen called the Environmental Health Department. I had bought a vacuum-packing machine some twenty years earlier. It had been a big decision, but I felt it would ensure that my customers got cooked meats and cheese as fresh as when they were newly cut. Some people wondered when we started the packing system, whether the goods would be fresh, and I was able to assure them that they would be. I had an assistant who cut all the meats and bacon, and she was the epitome of cleanliness, almost to perfection. The slicing machines were, of course, also kept spotlessly clean, for I always remembered that my reputation depended on the standard of the goods I sold. The meats and cheeses were cut in the back shop, and I had purchased a self-service refrigerator to display the goods.

We continued this operation for fifteen years, until the day an Environmental Health official came to me and said "We are not permitting you to carry on cutting meats in the atmosphere of the back shop." I asked why this decision had suddenly been made, since I had observed this practice for fifteen years. I also asked how many complaints had been received. When he told me that none had been made, I asked whether this really warranted a ban on what had been acceptable practice until now. "Others have to come up to standard, so you'll have to tell me what plans you have for improving the packing area, and I'll let you know if I accept them."

I had plans drawn up for an 8 foot by 4 foot enclosed area or 'house', with air ducts, and when this was passed, I had a joiner construct it. After its completion, the environmental health officer returned, and informed me that he was not accepting it now, and wanted this house to be 13 foot by 8 foot, with a wash-hand basin within the enclosed area. I had not had a basin incorporated within the existing house since there was a stainless steel wash-basin within 5 foot of it.

It was while I was thus disillusioned with the attitudes of our modern bureaucracy that I learned that for the first time in my life, a company wanted to purchase my shop. I suppose the strain and disappointment of the persecution I was undergoing made the decision easier, and I sold my business. It was a very emotional time, and the end of a greatly enjoyable working life.

As I look back at that time, the difficulties of keeping all things in order were more than surpassed by the satisfaction of knowing that I had never had one unprofitable year in business. From the first little shop, with three assistants, there had always been the delight of seeing growth and happiness, and that was what mattered most to me. To increase the turn-over of goods while being limited to the same selling space until I took over the old Holburn Bar had not been easy, but I had done it. The little prayer I had offered when I bought my first wee shop had been fully answered, and I had paid all my creditors their due.

I thought I would say 'thank you' to my customers so, as I had done every year in business, I gave away about £200 of gifts, and made up simple competitions with prizes displayed in the window. I invited customers to come and watch the draw, usually on a Tuesday morning - and the names and addresses of prize winners were then displayed in the window. It all added to the fun of life, for the business had been my whole life, with very few outside interests.

Another annual event had been the staff night out, which had begun as soon as I knew I could afford it, according to my trade returns. The staff were taken to a hotel by taxi, then on to a show, and then home after a cup of tea. It was the least I could do to repay their loyalty to me and the business. They always appreciated it. Appreciation came from my customers too, and so many have said how much they miss me in Holburn Street.

Looking back to the affair with the environmental health folk, I should heartily recommend to them a course on how to deal with traders, conducted by Albert Elrick. Now retired, Albert was an officer with the Weights and Measures Department, and although he had a mighty power over traders, his approach was commendable.

He was no soft touch, but he kept up standards without losing the human perspective. I wish these new environmental

A visit from Albert Elrick and his assistant

health people would learn from Albert, to recognise when traders are trying to do their best by their customers and the products they sell. I am far from being the only casualty of the Environmental Health Department, and I am saddened that Mr. Major has not, after all, endeavoured to keep the independent flag flying. If we were once a nation of shopkeepers, we are quickly becoming smaller and smaller in number.

The staff at 219 Holburn Street

When I left Holburn Street, I thanked the girls who had given such faithful service over the years and showed my appreciation by having small mementos inscribed for them:

Ethel - 26 years;
Betty (Robertson), Helen and Elizabeth - 23 years;
Betty (Smith) and Pat - 18 years;
Eileen- 13 years;
Audrey - 8 years.

It marked the end of a wonderful working relationship, with much satisfaction, and a great deal of happiness. Indeed, one young lass, who had been with me three years, left to enter the Nursing profession, and it was touching to read her letter when she left on my birthday, expressing her thanks for the happy years she had spent with me.

CHAPTER TWENTY ONE

New Beginnings –
The Ellon Stall

NOTHING EVER remains the same, and the New Market
building was to be rebuilt, necessitating a new site for the
Ellon Stall. It was no easy task, and after a lot of searching,
Charlie Alexander and I went to see the old Post Office premises in Allardyce Street, Stonehaven. It was anything but
inviting, with loose stones all over the floor, along with old
tiles. Apart from one good sized area the rest of the premises
consisted of a number of small rooms. I measured it out, and
reckoned there was a real possibility of some 2,000 square feet.
I told Charlie this would do, but as the Royal Hotel occupied
property above the place I reckoned it would take a lot of steel
to keep the hotel out of the shop.

My friend Alex Farquhar the builder came to the rescue
again, and thousands of pounds of steel gave us good sized
premises. With a lot of rooms above our part of the property
and adjacent premises, we had enough space for stock. Just as
with the old Holburn Bar, the front had to be taken out and
replaced with windows and doors. We laid the floor in terrazo
so that it was permanent and needed no maintenance apart from
cleaning. It took months to get the place in order, but we were
still trading in the New Market under limited time.

We had first option on a place within the Market when it

was rebuilt, but after meetings with the new owners and the City Assessors department, it was clear that the rents and rates would be prohibitive, and not for grocers' margins. With these margins anything from 11 to 19 percent, it would have taken all potential profit for rents and rates alone. With the 40 feet frontage of the Stonehaven property facing the square and car-park, I had no doubt that this was the place for our supermarket.

We were ready to open the first supermarket in Stonehaven, and if my shop had been the first self-service in Aberdeen, this was yet another first. For the big day, we asked Tom Nicol, from an old folks' home in Stonehaven to do the opening, and Charlie picked him up in his Rolls. Charlie thought he would have a word with customers as they entered the shop, but I told him he would have to make his welcome speech outside the shop before it opened. I'll never forget his saying "You spoil me," but I never really understood what he meant.

Charlie Alexander, though he was a millionaire, was not born with a silver spoon in his mouth. We had many conversations about things other than business, and I remember him once telling me about the time he was a farm worker. As was the custom with farm workers, he received a six-month pay, and when he had made his savings up to £100, he was left with half a crown to last him the next six months. "Mac," he told me, "I was determined not to be as poor as my father and mother." At the end of the next six months he still had part of the half-crown left, by various means, like getting a fellow farm worker to cut his hair with the horse clippers.

On another occasion, as a young lad, he was working away when the leading man at the farm hung him up by his heels on the back of the stable door. Years passed, and Charlie was now driving a lorry in partnership with his brother. He was carting sand from the Bridge of Don to a building site in Aberdeen. On the Ellon road Charlie noticed a workman coming from the town towards them on a bicycle. Charlie told his brother he wanted to leave early next morning so that he could speak to the man. Next day the lorry was beyond the houses on the Ellon road when the man appeared. Charlie got out of the lorry and spoke to him: "Do you know me? I remember you, and maybe you remember when you hung me up by the heels at the back of the stable door?" "Well," said Charlie "we're both men now, so you'd better get your jacket off." With great glee and satisfaction, Charlie told me "Mac, I gave him a damn good hiding, and told him to be careful how he treated young lads since they had a habit of growing up to be men."

Charlie introduced Tom Nicol to a fair crowd waiting outside and Tom officially opened the shop, where the usual boxes of fruit and bunches of flowers awaited. I organised a huge box of fruit for the home, which Tom took with him. Mrs Alexander said "Mac, what do I get?" "Mrs Alexander," I replied, "It's *all* yours." I'm sure she never wanted for anything, and she held more shares as a director than I did. It was a most successful opening, but I had no fears anyway, since it was the one and only supermarket in the town, and on a perfect site.

It was some years before we got any serious opposition, and any wee problems were ironed out without any harm to the business. We lost Ian as manager and appointed George Burnett who had worked in the Ellon Stall at the New Market. He was employed with a fairly large firm in the town, but we persuaded him to join us, and the following years were so successful that we planned an extension to the store, with the advantage of increasing the selling area by 850 square feet. Now we were able to bring the meat and bacon area up to the necessary requirements. The operation cost in the region of £50,000 and the supermarket was self-financing, which I thought was a terrific achievement.

The years passed and Charlie was now approaching 90 years of age. Mrs Alexander had died. The directors were now Charlie, his daughter Madge, George the manager and myself. A decision was taken at a meeting with Mr Levie, our secretary from Burnett and Reid, that a proposition was to be made so that George Burnett and his wife could take over the business. They had been such good friends to the firm that I was pleased their dedication and effort were to be rewarded. Acceptable terms were put on the table, and things were put in place for the take-over.

My first years in the firm, when I didn't receive director's fees, led many to say what a fool I was 'knocking my pan in' for Charlie Alexander. I replied that I was doing it for the girls who worked for us, who deserved proper reward for their efforts and without whom the shop could not operate. I was happy with the girls I interviewed for the shop when it opened, some of whom were there for fifteen to twenty years.

I eventually did get director's fees, but I have no regrets for anything I did - none at all. Being in association with a place which had been taken almost from bankruptcy to a valuable and viable concern was more than enough reward. My investment was £178, so all the criticising I had to endure did not worry me when the story had such a lovely ending.

CHAPTER TWENTY TWO

A Man of Leisure

I HAVE given the impression of obeying the work ethic to the exclusion of everything else, and it is certainly true that the challenges of building a business took up most of my time through the years. I did, however, have one leisure pursuit which provided challenges of its own.

A few years after I was established in the former Holburn Bar premises, Arthur and Alice Smart, from Mains of Cults, introduced me to the curling rink in Spring Garden. There was no fancy tuition or formality - you simply grabbed a brush, put your foot on a metal grid and hurled the stones along the ice. Almost from the first night I was hooked, and my interest has never waned. There was often a spare rink not required for competitions or league matches. With so much chance to get a bit of practice, the game became more and more interesting.

After a while Melville Watson asked Peter Clark of the Education Department and myself to join his team. Now we were 'curlers', and played in all the Donalds' Club league matches and competitions. Donalds' Club at this time had less than 20 members which grew to between 60 and 70 curlers. Besides games connected with the club, there were inter-city matches played all over Scotland, so that I have played in every Scottish city and had a great deal of fun and pleasure. One feature of some competitions was that visiting players were entertained by local teams when they got a free day.

There was a Grocers' Federation curling competition played annually, usually in Falkirk, Ayr in other years. There was a silver salver for the winners inscribed with the name of

L to R David Suttie, Ian Suttie, Duncan McGregor and Maisie Suttie

the town or district they represented. The only condition was that those who took part should be in some way connected with the grocery trade. Our team usually comprised of Jack and Maisie Settie, their sons Ian and David, and myself. Unsuccessful the first year, we won three times out of the next four, and it was good to see 'ABERDEEN' inscribed on the salver rather than Falkirk and District, or Perth. To date Aberdeen has won the competition ten times, been runners-up another ten, and the enjoyment of the day has never lessened. Mind you, we took part in this competition in the days when trains had dining cars, and this always added to the delight of the expedition.

Another competition to which we looked forward was the Perth Open Curling Competition which was again an annual event. We were in groups of four teams, but the competition was devised to guarantee each team three games which meant being away for a few days. After some years of simply enjoying our three games, we came top of our section. None of our team had expected this and had not made arrangements to stay longer, so we gave up our chance to carry on further in the competition. We might not have done much better but the experience would have been very worthwhile.

I won quite a lot of prizes for curling over the years, the best one for winning the Johnnie Walker Bonspiel at Donald's Ice Rink. It was a gallon bottle of Johnnie Walker's whisky on a stand; I have had it for 15 years now and it has remained untouched. I'm hoping that some day, on a special occasion, the contents can be enjoyed by many.

As the years passed, conditions at Donald's Ice Rink began to deteriorate - little wonder since the many years of supplying skating and curling facilities had taken their toll of the machinery. When the rink closed Aberdeen was left without an ice facility, and the best of the skaters had to travel quite considerable distances to practise, as had the curlers. It was not so handy, for the beauty of the local rink had been the ability to go for a game after work before going home. After a few years, however, Norman Cooper and a few other brave curlers decided to convert a building at Stoneywood into an ice rink. It must have caused them many a headache, but at last they had a first class facility with marked off rinks and excellent leisure facilities besides. Norman and his colleagues were all made permanent directors, and there were vacancies for three other directors who would serve for a three year period only. Pat Bruce, Jack Young and myself were asked to fill the vacancies. Our tasks were mainly in the fund raising field since too many were happy enough to use the facility, but not so ready to support it with their money.

Pat Bruce must receive the credit for raising many thousands of pounds, ably assisted by the lady curlers who thought up so many devices to get money. There were printed recipe books, coffee days, and especially their wonderful fashion shows - with many other fund raising schemes too numerous to mention. The men did their bit also, with cheese and wine evenings and boxing dinners. These dinners in particular have made thousands of pounds for the ice rink but with the burden of a huge loan, the tasks of management have been very difficult. We are still there, however, and the addition of skating and bowling in the same complex should provide future management with far fewer headaches.

The opening of the Stoneywood Ice Rink was performed by the Queen, and all the directors were presented to her. I haven't washed my hands since.

Boxing dinner at Stoneywood

PostScript

AS I look back over my life, it has been a great experience, and not so much pleasure for its own sake, but rather pleasure in work, and satisfaction with jobs well done.

My young days seem to have disappeared so quickly, without a lot of landmarks of outstanding interest. The unpleasantness of Bainshole was somewhat compensated by my uncle John being such a kind soul. I still meet some of the folks from the Glens of Foudland, and it's so good to reminisce, but, like all country places, many crofts and houses seem to have disappeared. I don't think there will be a dance and bun fight in the Glens school now. I don't know if my life would have changed so much had I remained at Bainshole instead of going south with the egg business.

My destiny in the army would not have been any different, and the war years, often with their day-to-day monotony, have been fairly well chronicled. Trying to keep clean with a mug of water per day meant a strict routine - wash teeth, shave then bathe. The essential need was for a sponge which, losing tank after tank, was difficult to purchase in the middle of the desert. I often recall the comment of the lads when I returned to the rear replenishing area after having another tank knocked out: "Nae you again, Mac. You're lucky not to catch it."

The interesting thing about my life is how experience has reshaped my thinking. I don't see many clouds, for there is this conscious feeling that I have so much for which to be grateful and for which I owe the world a great deal. I don't repeat every day "I should be grateful" - but there is the knowledge that I have been granted something which is not anyone's right so much as a blessing.

In the shop, when it was raining hard all day and customers were making remarks about how miserable it was, I automatically said "I can think of hundreds who would have loved to feel the water running down their faces, and you don't get another day in its place." I have a theory that everyone should come to work in the morning through a hospital ward, just to realise how lucky they are to have health and ability. We should never pass a precious day without being very conscious of the shadow we cast on life's path. We should try to make it pleasant since that same shadow can touch so many other lives. It's nice to think we can sow many kindly seeds and reap a harvest of lightening the burdens of others and making life more joyful.

I'm sure the influence of early years has a great bearing on our attitude to people and life. I am a regular church-goer, and believe that we should rightly feel humble; the most important things in life are gifts which no amount of money can buy. How often folk have said to me "I'm better than you and I don't go to church." I used to challenge them to imagine then, how much worse I might be if I didn't go to church. I offered part of this philosophy to my girls in the shop, asking them always to look after the poor old soul who only needs a couple of carrots, satisfying even that small need is important.

I recall an old lady who came to the shop every morning and who always looked quite ill. I began to chat to her each day and always remarked how much better she was looking with every passing day. I'm sure within a few days she actually felt better, and she was certainly much cheerier. The best thing for me has been to be able to get close to people, for there is so much good in folk which simply needs a little nourishment.

I have felt pride, such as when I bought my little shop at 202 Holburn Street, and when I opened the first self-service shop in Aberdeen with 612 sqare feet. What joy I felt in spite of not being able to broadcast my feelings in case anything went wrong. I feel a pride in the success of the conversion of the old Holburn Bar, and that I achieved it by my own decisions and plans. Yes and I am proud to have been a part of the Desert Rats, looking back on the strains and successes of two and a half years in the desert, six months in Italy, and the ten months in France after D-Day. I'll always remember the tank warfare, and Captain Thom who was such a genuine person, ready to pay the supreme sacrifice for his country and his beliefs. I think of him as we made those morning sorties at Knightsbridge to give protection for the squadron. Our troop was really on the altar of sacrifice, and all our three tanks were knocked out while the rest of the squadron tanks were saved. The one tank crew which was burned alive paid the price while the rest of us were made to constantly offer that price.

I think of the teaching of Jesus about the two men in the field when *one was taken and the other left.* I was left from that time of bloodshed and horror, and I have tried to show my thanks in what I have tried to achieve in life. One thing is certain and that is that one day we shall face the Master to account for our stewardship of life. I pray that He will say to me "Duncan, you've made good use of those bonus years I gave you." Amen to that.

Also available from Ardo

Green Heritage

This novel was written in the early thirties by
John R. Allan A successful young London business man
discovers his roots in Scotland's North East.

A Lucky Chap

The autobiography of Sir Maitland Mackie, who with his father
founded what has become the biggest farming business in
Scotland. It tells of eighty years of fun.

Farmer's Diary

*Charlie Allan records his struggles when he
returned to the family farm in 1989 after three years
in Kenya's Happy Valley. He tells how he got the farm going
again, tried to keep the banker happy and
re-established a place in the small North East
community of Methlick. Illustrations by Turnbull*

Volume II

*The continuing battle with the weather and bureaucracy
Charlie recounts fun with the Discussion Group
at the Salmon Inn where they met to blow about
crop yields or drown their sorrows when the weather won.*

Coming soon... Volume III
Further exploits of the Discussion Group

All available in the shops at £12.50
or direct from Methlick
please add £1 for postage.

Ardo Publishing Company Ltd.
Methlick, Aberdeenshire AB41 0HR